Subservience:

Political and Economic Decisions that Created a Global Black Underclass.

Two centuries ago, a former European colony decided to catch up with Europe. It succeeded so well that United States of America became a monster, the sickness and the inhumanity of Europe have grown to appalling dimensions. – Ibrahim Frantz Fanon

Imperialism leaves behind germs of rot which we must clinically detect and remove from our land but from our minds as well. – Ibrahim Frantz Fanon

The essence of neocolonialism is that the state which is subject to it is, in theory, independent and has all the trappings of international sovereignty. In reality it's economic system and thus its political system is directed from the outside. Hence, although political control had now ended, Africa still had to contend with colonial inequalities. – Kwame Nkrumah

Under its current form, that is imperialism-controlled, debt is a cleverly managed reconquest of Africa, aiming at subjugating its growth and development through foreign rules. Thus, each one of us becomes the financial slave, which is to say a true slave. – Thomas Isidore Noël Sankara

He who feeds you, controls you. – Thomas Isidore Noël Sankara

Most negro intellectuals simply repeat propaganda which is put out by people who have large economic and political interests to protect… At present time many of them find themselves in the humiliating position of running around the world telling Africans and others how well off negros are in the United States, and how well they are treated. – E. Franklin Frazier

European expansion to, and colonization of, Africa must be seen as an attempt to acquire political power, via colonization, that would be commensurate with, and further consolidate, its economic power at home. – Peter Ekeh

Perhaps the most extraordinary characteristic of current America is the attempt to reduce life to buying and selling. Life is not love unless love is sex and bought and sold. Life is not knowledge – save knowledge of technique, of science for destruction. Life is not beauty except beauty for sale. Life is not art unless its price is high, and it is sold for profit. All life is production for profit, and what is profit but for buying and selling again?" - W.E.B. Dubois

Racism… is a universal operating system of white supremacy and domination in which the majority of the worlds white people participate. – Dr. Frances Cress Welsing

For education among all kinds of men always has had, and always will have, an element of danger and revolution, of dissatisfaction and discontent. – W.E.B. Dubois

If you want to understand any problem in America, you need to focus on who profits from that problem, not who suffers from that problem. – Dr. Amos Wilson

Inequality can be done away with only by establishing a new society, where men and women will enjoy equal rights, resulting from an upheaval in the means of production and in all social relations. Thus, the status of the women will improve only with the system that exploits them. – Thomas Isidore Noël Sankara

The rulers of this country have always considered their property more important than our lives. – Assata Shakur

"Radical" is a label that is always applied to people who are endeavoring to get freedom. – Marcus Garvey

Why does the Black man say, "Freedom is doing what I want to do"? Why is it that "everything he wants to do" enriches the European? – Dr. Amos Wilson

…We don't hate white people, we hate the oppressor, whether he be Black, White, Brown, or Yellow." – Fred Hampton

Beware of Africans with American Dreams. – Jay Robb

People get used to anything. The less you think about your oppression, the more your tolerance for it grows. After a while, people just think oppression is the normal state of things. But to become free, you have to be acutely aware of being a slave. – Assata Shakur

African development is possible only on the basis of a radical break with the international capitalist system, which has been the principle agency of underdevelopment of Africa over the last five centuries. – Walter Rodney

When you talk about a revolution, most people think violence, without realizing that the real content of any type of revolutionary thrust lies in the principles and the goals that you are striving for, not in the way you reach them. – Angela Davis

We say we're not going to fight capitalism with black capitalism, but we're going to fight it with socialism. We're stood up and said we're not going to fight reactionary pigs and reactionary state's attorneys like this and reactionary state's attorneys like Hanrahan with any other reactions on our part. We're going to fight their reactions with all of us people getting together and having an international proletarian revolution." – Fred Hampton

The restitution of Africa's humanist and egalitarian principles of society require socialism. – Kwame Nkrumah

If one is truly a revolutionary, one must understand that one must take time out to study. Because revolutionary theories are based on historical analyses, one must study. – Kwame Ture

Contents

In Remembrance of Stephon Clark
Speech given in support of The California Act to Save Lives
March 6th, 2019

The District Attorney's press conference in which she dehumanized Stephon Clark was presented as if she was in front of a judge and jury; highlighting the contentions within his life as exculpatory findings suggesting he wanted to die. The students who walked out of class had a personal relationship with Stephon Clark. He was an Alumni of Sacramento Charter High School, he was a student at Sacramento City College, and he also touched the lives of many on the Campus of Sacramento State University. To that end, we must also dig deeper to the root of the turbulence in his life as highlighted by the District Attorney. The disparagement in education and development, particularly in Sacramento City Unified School district does not maximize its efficacy to foster in the development in its Black students. It perpetuates the school to prison pipeline highlighted by the way in which it failed Stephon Clark. In 2017 Sacramento City Unified School District averaged a number of 136 Black educators to 7552 Black students, equaling a teacher-student ratio of 1:55. Thus, echoing the cultural competency contentions and its correlation to the disparagement in their development by Sacramento Charter High School students. These concerns are not new, the ostracization of the Black community in education and development by city and state government predates the Civil Rights Movement. Our contentions with law enforcement predate our emancipation; stemming from the relationship between the slave and slave patrol. Anecdotally, it should be noted that California's penal code regarding police use of force has not been amended since 1872, 9 years after the signing of the emancipation proclamation.

50 years ago, the Black Panther Party for Self Defense marched onto the Capitol armed with weapons to protect themselves from police violence while addressing these very issues we are demanding today. Over-policing, the misuse of force, as well as educational disparagement. Last year, our fellow students and peers marched on the capitol in Washington DC to bring awareness to national gun reform in response to mass shootings taking place in schools across our nation. Today, we march to the state capitol to reiterate the demands and concerns of the Black Panther Party and add Police Gun Reform to the national discussion on gun laws. This issue is of top priority and has an extensive documented history of being brought to city, state and national representatives to no avail. The students will no longer wait. We demand that police use of force laws and policies are amended immediately!

National Lawyers Guild Speech
1/14/2020

Theory without practice is just as incomplete as practice without theory. The two have to go together.

These words from sister Assata Shakur should be the impetus to any activism, however it must be coupled with the dialectics of decolonization as defined by Algerian revolutionary and psychologist Frantz Fanon; in which he said: Imperialism leaves behind germs of rot which we must clinically detect and remove from our land but from our minds as well.

Therefore, decolonization is not something that happens only externally, but internally as well. The process of decolonization needs to occur in our minds, in our relationships, in our coalitions, in our communities, and in our society. Our lived experiences differ in that this imperialist nation has never succeeded any power, in that the settler colony that is the United States continues to propagandize it's need for colonial systems of control and continues to be autopoietic or self-maintaining despite us chipping away at the power structure. The egregiousness of western culture has created a society where alienation is normal and ubiquitous, yet we wonder why we have problems like mass shootings which are the reactions by those pushed to the furthest point on the peripheral border of our society and facing extreme alienation. I'm not sure if it is really even possible to shift the consciousness of an imperial society that is the United States, however revolutionary humanitarian change is needed within our local spaces. Not humanitarian change whose gaze is Eurocentric, but real third world centered afro-centric humanitarianism.

I must commend those who have aided in our efforts of decolonizing our communities. We cannot achieve this alone, and the importance of collation building cannot be stressed any further. But these coalitions must understand that the quandary of colonized people can only be solved by colonized people. And it is not because of the colonized that we are in this predicament but because of the colonizers. You see, revolutionary humanitarianism is of interest to all of us, as Aime Cesair has poetically delineated the concept of the boomerang effect of colonialism. Which when applied today shows how these institutions such as the prison system, law enforcement, the education system, the economic system, and all the systems deriving from colonialism which dehumanize the colonial subjects actually causes the colonizers to psychologically view themselves as less than human as a result of a dehumanized environment.

In the words of my beloved sister Assata Shakur:

This is the 21st century and we need to redefine revolution. This planet needs a people's revolution. A humanist revolution. Revolution is not about bloodshed or about going to the mountains and fighting. We will fight if we are forced to, but the fundamental goal of revolution must be peace.

We need a revolution of the mind. We need a revolution of the heart. We need a revolution of the spirit. The power of the people is stronger than any weapon. A people's revolution can't be stopped. We need to be weapons of mass construction. Weapons of mass love. It's not enough just to change the system. We need to change ourselves. We have got to make this world user friendly.

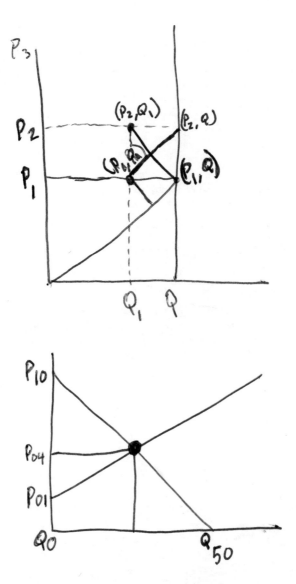

Section I
Articles

Not So Democratic "Democratic" Politics
By: Khalil Ferguson

During the post-reconstruction era of the United States, the Democratic Party has been perceived as the party of moral and civil progression. However, historically and contemporarily, the Democratic Party has been one of the largest impediments to substantial Black progression. Frantz Fanon, in his book *Towards the African Revolution* highlights how the Democratic Party in France attempted to aid Algeria in the Franco-Algerian war by offering strides for decolonization under France's terms while rejecting Algerian sentiment for complete liberation because it repudiated France's control as well as any quasi-dominance within the nation-state. Analogous to the condition of Black people in America, progress has only come on the condition that it did not alter the power structure. This is not highlighting the Republican Party as being a beacon of progress for the Black community, but merely pointing out the ostensible characteristic of the Democratic Party in the hindrance of Black progression.

The parallels between The French Democratic Party attempts of cooptation and American Democratic Party cooptation have been demonstrated in the form of economic ostracization. Since the emancipation of the slaves, Black economic prosperity has either been recused or preemptively denied. This has been at the hands of ostensibly progressive, moderate democrats. Again, historically and contemporarily, moderate democrats have been catalysts minimizing Black social and economic mobility.

The Freedmen's Bureau Bill, which established the Freedmen's Bureau on March 3rd, 1865, was initiated by President Abraham Lincoln and was intended to last for one year after the end of the Civil War. An excerpt taken from Edward McPherson, *The Political History of the United States of America, During the Period of Reconstruction* highlights President Andrew Johnson's role in its recusal:

> *"The Bureau was designed to provide economic and social assistance to 'Freedmen and Refugees' throughout the United States under the direction of the Secretary of War and newly appointed commissioners. The Second Freedmen's Bureau Bill, along with a Civil Rights Act, passed Congress with unanimous Republican support. The bills modified presidential reconstruction by providing more federal assistance and oversight for Unionists and freed slaves in the Southern states. Johnson surprised the legislators by vetoing both bills, rejecting a conciliatory draft message prepared by Secretary of State Seward in favor a strongly worded message denouncing congressional policy."*

Again, this is not intended to highlight the ostensible benevolence by the Republican Party (they have also been a great hindrance), but to emphasize the egregious propensities of moderate Democrats dilapidating Black progression. Upon emancipation, after President Lincoln was killed, Vice President Andrew Johnson assumed the presidency role. However, under President Johnson the Freedman's Bureau was recused, land confiscated during the civil war by the union was returned to former slave owners, and political power was restored to southern Democrats.

After the promulgation of the Federal Reserve Act in 1913 under President Woodrow Wilson, the Federal Farm Loan Act was signed into law in 1916. Appeasing the agricultural economy of the south, this bill was passed to provide capital to the agricultural sector which had become capital intensive in order to proctor sustainable growth. For Black people in the south, agriculture was their main source of capital inflow, however perpetual indebtedness from the sharecropping system ensured their economic and social mobility remained stagnant. In addition, the land the former slaves acquired after the civil war was returned to the planter class, further lamenting Black subordination. President Wilson, in order to retain support from southern Democrats ensured capital from the Federal Loan Act would not be extended to Black farmers. Therefore, ostracizing them from upward economic mobility.

President Franklin Delano Roosevelt was responsible for the inception of New Deal Reform programs which helped bring the country out economic turmoil under the guild of Keynesian economics. Keynesian economic thought theorizes that government intervention in the market would allow for the greatest marginal utility among the people, while also promoting domestic economic stability, and full employment. Under President Roosevelt the Federal Housing Administration was conceived in 1934. Through this, government subsidized mortgage packages were created to aid in the proliferation of home ownership; a process called suburbanization in political science discourse. Black people during this time period were isolated from upward economic mobility. Through means of *de jure* and *de facto* economic practices, Black households were isolated from attaining government subsidized mortgages. Mehrsa Baradaran in her book *The Color of Money* asserts that between 1934 and 1968, 98 percent of FHA loans went to white Americans. Thus, New Deal reform programs engendered a thriving white middle class, while cementing Black ghetto subservience.

Both Martin Luther King Jr. and Malcolm X highlighted the contentions between the Democratic Party, moderates, and the Black community. MLK Jr. in his Birmingham jail letter expresses his scorn towards the moderate politician:

> *"First, I must confess that over the past few years I have been gravely disappointed with the white moderate. I have almost reached the regrettable conclusion that the Negro's great stumbling block in his stride toward freedom is not the White Citizen's Council-er or the Ku Klux Klanner, but the white moderate, who is more devoted to "order" than to justice; who prefers a negative peace which is the absence of tension to a positive peace which is the presence of justice; who constantly says: "I agree with you in the goal you seek, but I cannot agree with your methods of direct action"; who paternalistically believes he can set the timetable for another man's freedom; who lives by a mythical concept of time and who constantly advises the Negro to wait for a "more convenient season." Shallow understanding from people of good will is more frustrating than absolute misunderstanding from people of ill will. Lukewarm acceptance is much more bewildering than outright rejection."*

Throughout the duration of the civil rights movement, socioeconomic suppression of Black people proliferated. The welfare reform programs conceptualized by President Lyndon Johnson cascaded into the war on welfare, the war on drugs, and subsequently the war on crime. Although, these programs were started by Republican politicians, the rhetoric was echoed by Democratic politicians such as President Jimmy Carter, President Bill Clinton and presidential candidate Joe Biden. Joe Biden and President Bill Clinton were instrumental in the socioeconomic suppression of Blacks. Joe Biden initially introduced the three strikes Bill, and President Clinton signed it. The Three Strikes Bill has been studied and cited as a large proponent in the exacerbation of the mass incarceration of Black people in the United States.

A centrist politician whose stance on reparations for Black people was neoliberal economic investment into Black communities. Barack Obama, self-proclaimed as being less liberal than President Nixon, did little to augment the socioeconomic status of Black people. From the global perspective Obama perpetuated global white supremacy despite being "African American". President Obama would precipitously increase the amount of drone strikes in the Middle East relative to his predecessor under the guise of the War on Terror, which spiked the number of civilian casualties 100x; these bombings, according to The Geneva Convention of 1977 are also delineated as violations of international law under Article 51 section 5:

5. Among others, the following types of attacks are to be considered as indiscriminate:

(a) an attack by bombardment by any methods or means which treats as a single military objective a number of clearly separated and distinct military objectives located in a city, town, village or other area containing a similar concentration of civilians or civilian objects; and

(b) an attack which may be expected to cause incidental loss of civilian life, injury to civilians, damage to civilian objects, or a combination thereof, which would be excessive in relation to the concrete and direct military advantage anticipated.

His ordeals on the continent of Africa would also undermine the autonomy of a sovereign state under the guise of "Humanitarian Intervention". Corroborating with NATO, President Obama, and Secretary of State Hillary Clinton would continue the persecution of Muammar Gathafi. What has now been substantiated as being for strategic occupation of oil reserves under the proxy of General Hiftar. Retrospectively, uncovered plans display Gathafi was planning to create a Libyan currency pegged to their gold reserves, drastically challenging United States imperialism in the global market.

Former San Francisco District Attorney Kamala Harris, who was also California's Attorney General has played a role in the perpetual disenfranchising relationship between the Black community and the prison industrial complex. Senator Kamala Harris during her time as a prosecutor took stances on policies that have roots in the aforementioned socioeconomic "wars". The most prolific stance Senator Harris took was championing the controversial anti-truancy law which sought to reduce the number of children missing school by imposing fines or jail time upon parents. Additionally, Senator Harris' "Smart on Crime" rhetoric had nuances of "Tough on Crime" rhetoric expressed during the 1990's. It does not help that felony conviction rates rose from 52 percent to 67 percent in three years during her time as San Francisco's District Attorney.

Assembly Bill 392 authored by Assembly members Weber and McCarty has been introduced as the *Act to Save Lives*. Police in California kill community members at a rate 37 percent higher than the national average, per capita, and several of our state's police departments have among the highest rates of killings in the country. The excessive use of force by police officers is ubiquitous throughout the United States. AB 392 seeks to amend California's penal code regarding police use of force standard which has not been amended since 1872, nine years after the signing of the emancipation proclamation.

Immediately, the bill faced opposition from moderate democrats who seek to uphold the status quo of the current use of force standards. Senate Bill 230 has been co-authored by approximately 16 moderate democrats who seek to increase the training of police officers, but not bind any misconduct to legal statute. This is erroneous as it does not enforce any accountability standards for officers who exert an excessive amount of force.

In the case of Willie McCoy who was killed by Vallejo Police Department while awakening from sleep in his car, six officers fired 25 bullets into the car, in the direction of McCoy, parallel to the 20 shots fired at Stephon Clark. Both parties died as a result of gunshot wounds. To this end, it is clear that moderate democrats have played a pervasive role in the progression Black social and economic mobility. Much like MLK Jr. said "the Negro's great stumbling block in his stride toward freedom is not the White Citizen's Council-er or the Ku Klux Klanner, but the white moderate, who is more devoted to "order" than to justice…" It is of great importance that this trend end. It is tiring to have our oppression continually politicized, since the Civil Rights Movement the passage of legislation to create a more equitable society has been cut short because of the moderate politician creating marginal legislative losses for Black progression.

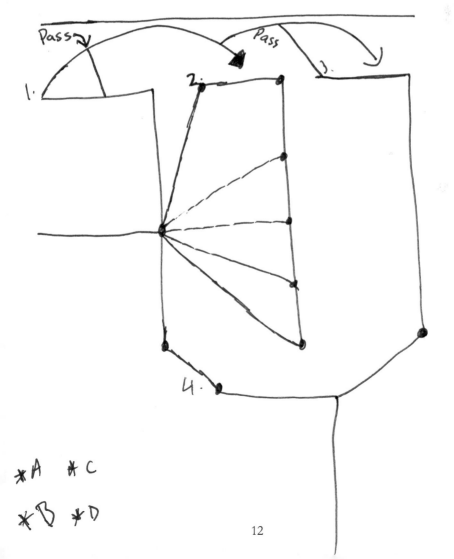

Neocolonialism in Sacramento
By: Khalil Ferguson

The Algerian revolutionary Frantz Fanon defines colonialism as "...the conquest of a national territory and the oppression of a people... Within the context of occupied territory, colonialism comes forth as dichotomizing force, enforcing oppressor and oppressed roles..." this definition allows us to examine the basis for neocolonialism which has been substantiated by Kwame Nkrumah, the first President of Ghana; he contends, "[T]he essence of neocolonialism is that the state which is subject to it is, in theory, independent and has all the trappings of international sovereignty. In reality it's economic system and thus its political system is directed from the outside." Within the Black community, gentrification can be viewed as neocolonialism, as it stems from the lack of political and economic control over the neighborhood which we reside in. Gentrification is rampant throughout the United States, particularly California, and more microcosmically in the City of Sacramento. The examination of neocolonialism is apparent in Sacramento through urban developmental policies guided by the auspices of laissez-faire market fundamentalism and macroeconomic regulatory premises, otherwise known as economic neoliberalism.

Gentrification in Sacramento and Neocolonialism on the continent of Africa stem from the same neoliberal policies and have the same degradational effects. The erosion of communal relations and the displacement of low-income individuals are an afterthought in place for urban development policies that seek to attract direct investment in an attempt to revitalize the community. Therefore, it can be observed that community members who reside in the jurisdiction of the specific areas have no economic or political control over policies that affects their livelihood, in line with the premise of neocolonialism outlined by Kwame Nkrumah.

As I have lived in Sacramento and attended Sacramento State, studying Economics and International relations, I have noticed distinct similarities between the imposition of free market policies in the political economic sphere that aid in the exacerbation of socioeconomic issues for Black people domestically and globally.

The conditions faced by my people are the results of racist policies such as redlining, segregation, and over-policing. Legitimized by the state apparatus and capitalist finance institutions, these de jure and de facto practices created a dependency relationship between us and the state. As I observed the history of Oak Park and the characteristics of suburbanization leading to white flight, I found that the same colonial systems of control were used to mitigate problems in the neighborhood as were used in colonial Africa – a punitive and militarized criminal justice system. In addition, I have found that the ramifications of these policies are what have created the environment allowing for gentrification.

The premise for the economic neoliberal politic is financial liberalization, privatization, slashing of government spending (austerity), and the cultivation of a business climate ripe for inward capital investments. In Africa, the imposition of Structural Adjustment Programs (SAPs) allowed for the privatization and commandeering of the African Economy under the purview of a free market-oriented economy. Similarly, these policies are apparent when analyzing gentrification here in Sacramento. The idea of New Market Tax Credits (NMTCs), and Opportunity Zones, are propensities contributing to growing gentrification. In fact, the propagation of Opportunity Zones can be traced to Richard Nixon who was a supporter of laissez-faire economics. The rhetoric reinforces trickledown economics; contending that the means to lift populations out of poverty was to incentivize, and encourage private developers to invest in downtrodden communities (those affected by redlining, over-policing, and mass incarceration), resulting in the ostensible creation of jobs while the developer benefits from deferring taxes on capital gains throughout the longevity of investment holdings. However in 1995, a study conducted by the British government on the efficacy of enterprise zones concluded that tax-break incentivized policies do work to spur investment, but do not create jobs and do not lift people out of poverty. Additionally, an article posted by _Forbes_ reinforces the statement that financial gains of Opportunity Zones largely benefit the investor relative to the community.

In my analysis, it came as no surprise that state designated Opportunity Zones are profound throughout Oak Park, an area which has already been affected by gentrification, as well as Del Paso Heights.

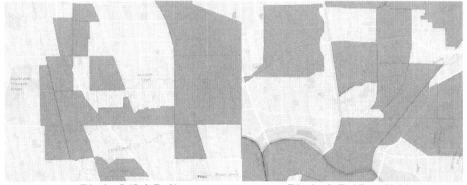

District 5 (Oak Park)   District 2 (Del Paso Heights)

Already, the consequences of these neoliberal policies appear in the disproportionate amount of Black people within the homeless population. A recent article published by the _SacBee_ shows how Black people, although making up 13 percent of the county's population, makeup 34 percent of the homeless population. This is the result of rising rents associated with redevelopment, pressure from migration from the Bay Area, and the inflation of prices on consumer goods accompanied by stagnant wages. Since displacement is inherent to gentrification – by definition, the removal of a lower class for a more affluent group of people, the connection between colonial domination of a territory and gentrification of a community is inextricably linked to neoliberal-neocolonial policies.

From Nixon, to Clinton, to Obama, and finally Trump the rhetoric surrounding Opportunity Zones has been reified despite having displayed perpetual shortcomings for Black people. This economic stance is also counterintuitive as low income community's makeup some of the largest consumer bases; a better strategy would be to directly invest into these consumer demographics in a more bubble-up economic manner. As a region we need to be more intentional, and inclusive when planning to develop areas that are composed of marginalized individuals. Bringing these populations from the periphery of our economy to the core should be the priority of both the public and private sector if we are to end the oppression of Black lives under this neoliberal economic regime.

Section II
Essays

A Brief Timeline of Black Economic Subjugation

The asymmetric economic relationship between the Black community and the white community is imbedded in the foundation of the United States. Since the promulgation of the Constitution the accumulation of wealth into white families has come at the expense of Black subservience. The dichotomy between the slave owner and the slave precipitated the polarized class relations between the Black community and the white community. While chattel slavery would be the catalyst for the perpetual economic subjugation of Black people in the American economy, class relations and wealth disparities would be exacerbated during the suburbanization period and President Roosevelt's New Deal programs. Economic isolation during suburbanization solidified the Black community's place in the lower-working class. The exportation of Black labor, and exploitation of capital reified poverty and led to the underdevelopment of Black neighborhoods. Under President Lyndon Baines Johnson, the War on Poverty was conceptualized. However, the programs which were conceived in an effort to alleviate poverty were counterintuitive and resulted in the curation of the War on Crime. The War on Crime disproportionately affected the Black community; resulting in the over-policing of Black neighborhoods and successively the mass incarceration of Black individuals. To this end, the lower-class status of Black people in the United States was promulgated during the antebellum period, which would be cemented during suburbanization, exploited during the Civil Rights Movement, and perpetuated contemporarily.

Although the Constitution of the United States was signed in 1787, profit earnings off slave labor had already been utilized. According to Sven Beckert in the *Empire of Cotton*, cotton as a commodity became a very lucrative not only domestically, but internationally as well. The southern region particularly made exponential profits within the cotton market because of the exploitation of slave labor and the amount of arable land that was accessible. In 1786 the United States began to recognize the lucrative potentiality of cotton with the conception of mechanized cotton textile production in the United Kingdom (Beckert, 101). This would cause the rapid expansion of the domestic cotton market to rely on more slaves to extend its profit. In fact, the states of Georgia and North Carolina in the 1790s saw a dramatic increase in their slave population. In Georgia during the 1790s, the slave population nearly doubled, to sixty thousand. Over twenty years in North Carolina, the slave population increased from twenty-one thousand in 1970 to seventy thousand (Beckert, 103). The reification of lower-class status of Black slaves emanates from their utilization as property and financial instruments. The three-fifths compromise recognized them only as voting instruments to assist the political power of the planter class. Additionally, the economic utilization of slaves came in the form of collateral or property to be loaned. Beckert highlights "since the expansion of the cotton agriculture depended on the advance of credit, sometimes secured by mortgages on slaves, most of which derived from the London money market, its patterns now followed the competitive logic of markets rather than the whimsy of regional circumstance…" (Beckert, 116-117). Thus, a display of the aggrandization of Black lower-class status being exploited for profit. Beckert reifies "It was on the back of cotton, and thus on the backs of slaves, that the United States' economy ascended into the world." (Beckert, 119). This relationship would only precipitate the economic suppression of the Black community post-emancipation.

The post-war reconstruction era was a time in which the United States' economy experienced its greatest marginal rate of growth. Sparked by the Keynesian economic ideology, President Franklin Delano Roosevelt implemented New Deal reform programs. Keynesian economic thought theorizes that government intervention in the market would allow for the greatest market utility among the people (Baradaran, 67.) These programs were responsible for the augmentation of public housing programs which were subsidized by the federal government. Additionally, this economic ideology was responsible for the subsidizing of government backed mortgage securities, and essentially the proliferation of home ownership throughout the United States, referred to as suburbanization. Conversely, the Black community would be ostracized from participating in this economic growth. Because of the economic ideology of the United States allowing for government intervention in the markets, it can be substantiated that the Black community became economically deprived as a result of *de jure* and *de facto* economic policies.

The underwriting manual of the Federal Housing Administration imposed a number of "economic" ordinances which had racial undertones and reinforced segregation. An interview done by Terry Gross from *National Public Radio* and Richard Rothstein, author of *The Color of Law* illustrates how the FHA underwriting manual subverted the economic bearings of the Black community: "the most important role of the Federal Housing Administration was it subsidized mass-production builders of entire subdivisions, entire suburbs. And it did so with a requirement that no homes be sold to African-Americans and that every home in these subdivisions had a clause in the deed that prohibited resale to African-Americans." To this end, a report taken using statistics from the *1989 Survey of Consumer Finances* highlighted for "most middle-class families, wealth is closely tied to the value of their homes." It is because of policies of this nature, accompanied by redlining, and predatory installment loans that the Black community saw its capital leave its neighborhoods, and essentially became underdeveloped. Additionally, the expropriation of Black capital would result in the dilapidation of housing and living standards, as well as the propagation of poverty. It also must be noted that this economic isolation has largely contributed to the racial wealth gap. Mehrsa Baradaran, author of *The Color of Money*, maintains the notion that this isolation of Black economic growth in conjunction with robust white economic growth made Black ghettos permanent, juxtaposed to the thriving white middle class (Baradaran, 103). In support, Baradran substantiates the claim by highlighting the statistics in which ninety-eight percent of FHA loans between 1934 and 1968 went to White Americans (Baradaran, 108). Thus, solidifying the lower-class status of the Black household.

Following the cementing of denigrated Black neighborhoods, as well as the proliferation of poverty in Black communities, the War on Poverty was bourgeoned by President Lyndon Baines Johnson. The intention was to create programs which would help alleviate the poverty in these communities. As a result, The Office of Economic Opportunity and Economic Opportunity Act were fashioned during the Civil Rights Movement. However, the programs focused on economic equality, and not equity. Had these programs been able to specifically bolster the economic prosperity of the Black community, and narrow the wealth gap, then it could be argued that racial tensions would not be as polarized as they are today. Emanating from these failures at economic equality and poverty repudiation was the War on Crime. The War on Crime successively led to the increased surveillance, and the over policing of Black neighborhoods (Baradaran, 155.) Instead of antiquating crime by tending to its roots – poverty, presidential campaigns exhorted – tough on crime – rhetoric which would lead to the promulgation of the Three Strikes Law by Joe Biden and signed by President Bill Clinton. The Three Strikes Law exploited the labor of Black communities by disproportionately funneling Black individuals into the prison industrial complex. Michelle Alexander, author of *The New Jim Crow*, details how the prison industrial complex is the institutionalism of slavery through the thirteenth amendment. Conclusively, this strategy ensures Black economic mobility remains suppressed, and the Black community remains impoverished, subjected to the lower-working class status.

The economic contentions between the white and Black races have historically been one sided. The subjugation of Black people in the United States has been democratized and institutionalized. Physical domination has transcended into democratic institutions which perpetuate economic subordination, and class inferiority. Upward economic mobility has been made almost unattainable because of the root in which Black subservience has been created and maintained. Chattel Slavery conceived the relationship, The New Deal cemented it, and the War on Poverty and Crime exploited it. Thus, highlighting the timeline of class oppression by the white race upon the Black race.

Wow!.

Bibliography

A 'Forgotten History' Of How The U.S. Government Segregated America [Interview by T. Gross]. (2017, March 3). Retrieved March 15, 2019, from https://www.npr.org/templates/transcript/transcript.php?storyId=526655831

Baradaran, M. (2019). The color of money: Black banks and the racial wealth gap. Cambridge, MA: The Belknap Press of Harvard University Press.

Beckert, S. (2015). *Empire of cotton: A global history*. New York: Knopf.

Rothstein, R. (2018). *The color of law: A forgotten history of how our government segregated America*. New York: Liveright Publishing Corporation, a division of W. W. Norton & Company.

Wolff, E. (1995, Summer). How the Pie is Sliced: Americas Growing Concentration of Wealth. Retrieved March 16, 2019, from https://prospect.org/article/how-pie-sliced-americas-growing-concentration-wealth#r-fig07

Oakland's White Flight back into the City:
Gentrification as a result of Historic Economic Suppression of Blacks

During the early 1900s, the United States saw a large migration of Blacks from the rural south to the industrial north. Wanting to escape Jim Crow and the violence surrounding it, also in search of better jobs in a larger economic area, Blacks migrated to large cities in the north. Even though the great depression put a stop to Black Migration in the 1920s, a second wave of Black migration began around 1940. During this time period, the United States was gearing for World War II, therefore manufacturing jobs were of abundance. Of the large cities that Black people migrated to, Oakland, California is a city who has historically faced racial conflict and political suppression. Oakland, before the great migration of Blacks, had a predominately white population. As Blacks poured into the city over the years, Oakland ultimately became prominently Black, however, they still remained powerless within politics. During the 1950s and 60s the creation of suburbs on the outskirts of large cities occurred. Subsequently this caused large migration of middle-class and upper middle-class whites from cities widespread throughout the United States, known as the "white flight". The surge came from the increasing desires for white people to escape life in the city and more importantly, separate themselves from Blacks who largely inhabited these areas, perpetuating segregation in the city. Since then, cities like Oakland who were once large hubs for industrial businesses, have lost their attraction and have faced economic blight. These cities have tried to restore their economy by redeveloping their downtown areas and increase housing prices in an effort to bring back more affluent residents. The inhabitants of these areas are minorities, primarily Black. Consequently, because Black people have little political and economic power in Oakland, they are ostracized from the urban renewal planning and subsequently become victims of gentrification. Even though gentrification man be spun as positive because with gentrification comes more money, renovation, trendy stores and eateries. The Oakland Wiki defines gentrification as the phenomenon of wealthier residents moving to poorer neighborhoods for the cheaper rent and in the process raising neighborhood property values, eventually pricing out previous residents who can no longer afford higher rents and cost of living so that they must move elsewhere.[1] Moreover, the gentrification of low and middle-income urban neighborhoods is nothing new. Economists and scholars believe the process happening today is occurring more rapidly than in the past.[2] A new "white flight" is happening, because large cities are becoming progressively attractive to those who once sought to separate themselves from the city and from Blacks.

Some of the most fundamental aspects affecting the wealth inequality gap between Blacks and whites are higher rates of unemployment for Blacks, which is twice the amount of whites, also structural factors such as accessibility to jobs and discrimination play a role in widening the inequality gap.[3] Black people in Oakland have been oppressed economically since their migration to the city. The changing pattern of urban geography in the 1960s further perpetuated their economic suppression. The deindustrialization within the center of the city along with rapid industrialization of the suburbs surrounding the city, redevelopment and urban renewal, and white flight enlarged the economic gap between Blacks and whites. They embedded in society the perpetuation of historical racial disparities, particularly the unequal distribution of jobs and resources between Black and white communities, between city and suburb, and the physical destruction of Black neighborhoods which led to the displacement of Black residents. Because of their

---

[1] "Staff Editorial: Bay Area Gentrification."
[2] Robbie Whelan. "The New Urban Pioneers: Companies Spruce Up Neighborhoods, Putting Gentrification in Overdrive."
[3] Deborah Bayliss. "Blacks and the Elusive Attainment of Economic Power."

ostracism from politics in Oakland, the policies passed, and programs created were not to the benefit of the Black population. Industrial locations, plans for urban renewal and redevelopment, urban and suburban tax structure, the War on Poverty, and public housing, and education became sites of the defining class and racial struggles of the 1950s, 1960s, and 1970s.[4] Furthermore, these programs also aided in the economic suppression of Black people in Oakland, as they failed to ensure the promise of democracy and opportunity.[5] West Oakland continued to face occupational market restrictions as West Oakland continued to be flooded with Black Migrants, mostly moving from Texas, Oklahoma, Louisiana, and Arkansas. Upon migrating to the city Black workers still faced occupational disparities.[6] In 1960, among men, transportation, shipbuilding, light assembly and construction, provided the bulk of employment, and, two in three Black employees were in a semiskilled, unskilled, or service position.[7] However, one out of four Black young workers younger than twenty years old could not find employment, a rate that was twice as large as the general population.[8] Thus, data suggest that young workers, as well as women and newcomers, had trouble finding work because nearly all entry level positions were closed to them, and industries that typically hired young workers did not hire Black workers.[9]

By the middle of the 1960s, Oakland's southern outer border was dominated, by a string of low-tax industrial and residential suburbs that became, magnets for drawing people and capital away from Oakland (Milpitas, San Leandro, Fremont, and Hayward).[10] Consequently, contemporary gentrification results can be derived from the beginning of

---

[4] Robert Self. "“To Plan Our Liberation”." p.759-92
[5] Robert Self. "“To Plan Our Liberation”." p.759-92
[6] Ibid...,
[7] Ibid...,
[8] Ibid...,
[9] Ibid...,
[10] Ibid...,

urban redevelopment projects in the 1950's.[11] These projects were sponsored by the city under federal urban renewal laws, with the intentions of destroying older housing facilities in order to reinvigorate local neighborhood spaces.[12] The spaces destroyed for the purpose of reestablishing economic vitality were frequently spaces largely inhabited by Blacks.[13] Oakland politicians wanted to bring money back to the city of Oakland as well as increasing its economic prosperity during a time of decentralization and suburbanization. Aimed at bringing affluent residents back to the city, this resulted in the construction of three massive federal highways through West Oakland, vigorous redevelopment and containerization of the port in the 1960s, and the creation of the Bay Area Rapid Transit System (BART).[14] However, the combination of these projects cost West Oakland ten thousand housing units in one decade, that displaced local residents from the area.[15] With the rise of the Black Panthers and their ability to mobilize Black people, politics in Oakland shifted to become more intuitive to the needs of the Black community. This lasted for two decades until the election of Jerry Brown as mayor of Oakland.

Jerry Brown continued the process of gentrifying Oakland, he wanted to revitalize the downtown area of Oakland, as well as building more homes in the downtown area that would attract ten thousand more residents to the city. He stated he intended to bring back ten thousand of those whites among the millions who had joined the great exodus outward.[16] Brown's "exodus" simply is a code word for "white flight," a term referring to those whites who fled America's cities to avoid desegregated schools and all other forms of social integration with Blacks.[17] He calls them and their lost consumer dollars back with

---

[11] Robert Self. "'To Plan Our Liberation''." p.759-92
[12] Ibid...,
[13] Ibid...,
[14] Robert Self. "'To Plan Our Liberation''." p.759-92
[15] Ibid...,
[16] Elaine Brown. "Stop the Whitewashing of Oakland District 3."
[17] Ibid...,

the promise to get rid of the impoverished Blacks from whom they fled.[18] Jerry Brown capitalized on the trend that many politicians and researchers believed that residential housing was the key to revitalizing urban areas. In a 1995 review of downtown redevelopment efforts, seven strategies were found with regards to urban redevelopment.[19] Those seven strategies included, supporting retail venues, office complexes, waterfront development, and pedestrian enhancement.[20] These strategies set the tone to make urban cities more attractive, however, these redevelopment plans typically come in conjunction with the ostracism of Black people who aren't regarded in redevelopment planning. Black leaders and communities largely began to form distrust with Jerry Brown, as he alienated progressive Black leaders, causing them to refer to his policies as "Jerryfication".[21] Jerry Brown's strategy to revitalize Oakland did not include the residents of Oakland, he did not believe the stimulation of their economic condition would cure Oakland of its economic blight.[22] In an interview with the New York Times he stated: "We needed housing and not just for people that are hanging on or people who live on subsidies, but people who have disposable income that can go to the art galleries and restaurants."[23] Indicative of his intentions and how he aimed to achieve them. Jerry Brown did not believe that Blacks moving out of Oakland was a city problem, he saw it as regional problem as more Blacks were fleeing Richmond and San Francisco at larger rates in search of better housing values.[24] Brown stated that Oakland gained 27,000 people in the 1990s, however the percentage of Black decreased in the city from 45% to 35% according to the 2000 census.[25]

---

[18] Elaine Brown. "Stop the Whitewashing of Oakland District 3."
[19] Jessica Sheldon. "Going Uptown in Downtown Oakland: Market-Rate Housing as a Redevelopment Tool."
[20] Ibid…,
[21] Jessica Sheldon. "Going Uptown in Downtown Oakland: Market-Rate Housing as a Redevelopment Tool."
[22] Ibid…,
[23] Zusha Elinson. "As Mayor, Brown Remade Oakland's Downtown and Himself."
[24] Ibid…,
[25] Ibid…,

Because of Jerry Brown's introduction of residential housing into Oakland, many investors have begun their own attempts of residential redevelopment. Buying land, abandoned homes, or foreclosed houses, investors seek to increase the housing prices of not only the houses they buy, but the neighborhood they invest in. Thus, driving up housing prices for the neighborhood and the residents that occupy them. Real-estate firms say they need to spiff up neighborhoods to make their investments pay off. Jim McClelland, Chief executive of Mack Cos questioned why investors wouldn't want to further invest in the appeal of a neighborhood: "If your play is for long-term appreciation, versus just flipping the houses, wouldn't you want to improve the properties and make the area more desirable?"[26] A study conducted in 2012 by the Urban Strategies Council, an advocacy organization based in Oakland, found that between 2007 and 2011, 10,508 homes in the city went through foreclosure, and 42% were acquired by investors.[27] Because of its access to San Francisco, being one BART stop away from getting into the city, West Oakland has become a popular area for investors and redevelopment. One of the biggest investors in Oakland is Mr. Sullivan's REO Homes.[28] He acquired more than 200 homes in Oakland in 2008, with most of them being in West Oakland.[29] In addition to the investments, new, trendy restaurants have opened recently, and the neighborhood is getting younger and more ethnically diverse as more-affluent white and Asian renters move in. Because of investors, the rent for surrounding area has skyrocketed. According to the report released in 2013 at the city's Community and Economic Development Committee (CED) meeting, new rents in crime-heavy neighborhoods are rising to $2,200 per month.[30]

---

[26] Robbie Whelan. "The New Urban Pioneers: Companies Spruce Up Neighborhoods, Putting Gentrification in Overdrive."
[27] Robbie Whelan. "The New Urban Pioneers: Companies Spruce Up Neighborhoods, Putting Gentrification in Overdrive."
[28] Ibid...,
[29] Ibid...,
[30] Ibid...,

And even though the numbers of foreclosures in Oakland are decreasing, those who are affected have lived in their homes for 10 or more years.[31] Further displacing long standing residents. The effects of spiked housing prices have affected the City of Oakland all over, such as the Oakland hills, West Oakland and, Lake Merritt. Consequently, this has driven home buyers and renter to look for more affordable housing in East Oakland.[32] Because of this influx of demand, residents of East Oakland are slowly being coerced out of their neighborhoods with no substitute place to live.[33]

Also aiding in the rapid occurrence of gentrification in Oakland is the enforcement of gang injunctions in predominately Black low-income neighborhoods. Oakland has tried to enact gang injunctions in the city since the mid 90's, initially dismissed as unconstitutional, they were deemed legal in 1997 by the California State Supreme Court.[34] In 2009, City Attorney John Russo (elected under the mayor-ship of Jerry Brown) pushed to have an injunction filed members of the "North Side Oakland" gang in an area predominately inhabited by Blacks, that neighbored Berkeley and Emeryville.[35] It has been pointed out that he failed to mention that the injunction zone was located next to an already gentrified Temescal district.[36] Months later the City Attorney's office proposed a second injunction aimed at 40 members of the Norteños gang in a 450-block area of Fruitvale, a district that has been traditionally Latino.[37] A large problem with the enforcement of these injunctions is that, they did not coincide with Oakland Police Department's "hotspot enforcement" which is meant to targets areas with higher and

---

[31] Ken A. Epstein. "Oakland Rents Rise Astronomically, Long-Time Home Owners Face Foreclosure."
[32] "Gentrification Displaces Oakland Residents."
[33] Ibid...,
[34] Erik K. Arnold. "Oakland Gang Injunctions: Gentrification or Public Safety?"
[35] Erik K. Arnold. "Oakland Gang Injunctions: Gentrification or Public Safety?"
[36] Ibid...,
[37] Ibid...,

more frequent incidents of violent crime.[38] Actually, OPD's data showed that the city's

worst hotspots were located outside of the injunction zones.[39] And according to the

OPD's own statistics, violent crime actually rose in the NSO area after the injunction was

granted.[40] The conclusion has been made that the ulterior motive of the gang injunctions is

to remove low income residents and make neighborhoods more attractive to affluent

home buyers.[41] According to George Galvis of Communities United for Restorative Youth

Justice (CURYJ), "Gang injunctions are very effective tools for areas ripe for

gentrification."[42] Top criminologist Dr. Barry Krisberg informs the public of a strategy

called "privileged adjacency" which is a pattern of using gang injunctions to benefit nearby

affluent areas.[43] This is done by displacing poor and working Black and Latino families

from their homes and communities.

As Black people migrated into the City of Oakland from southern states in search

of jobs, and also to escape the Jim Crow laws, they were met with more systematic forms

of segregation. While it was not enforced by law in California that segregation was

mandatory, societal norms and economic inequalities perpetuated segregation in the city.

Occupational restrictions made it hard for Black people to work and even gain any

economic leverage, thus suppressing them. Federal programs and projects backed by the

federal government also aided in the disenfranchisement of Black Communities. Their

goals were to revitalize the economy of Oakland by redeveloping areas of Oakland to

influence more affluent residents back into the city. However, the implementation of the

programs was often accompanied with the misfortune of Black Communities. After the

[38] Erik K. Arnold. "Oakland Gang Injunctions: Gentrification or Public Safety?"
[39] Ibid...,
[40] Ibid...,
[41] Ibid...,
[42] Ibid...,
[43] Ibid...,

twenty years of Black political activism, Oakland's redevelopment and gentrification process was continued by Jerry Brown. Jerry Brown redevelopment efforts brought 27,000 people to the city of Oakland during the 1990s, but it also caused the percentage of Black People to drop from 45% to 35%. Jerry Brown also alienated Black leaders and Business owners who criticized Brown, because his politics did not elevate the Black Community. Furthermore, during Jerry Brown's time as mayor, John Russo was elected to City Attorney, supported by Brown he contributed to the gentrification process by filing gang injunctions in minority neighborhoods. Lastly, economic suppression of Black Communities and redevelopment efforts beginning in the 1950's, has created a climate for Black people to not have economical leverage to prevent themselves from becoming victims of gentrification, which was perpetuated by Jerry Brown, thus we have a mass exodus of Black people moving out of the city and a mass migration of Whites and Asians into Oakland.

Bibliography

"Blacks Grill Mayor Jerry Brown." *Sun Reporter,* Jan 24, 2002.
   http://proxy.lib.csus.edu/login?url=https://search-proquest-
   com.proxy.lib.csus.edu/docview/366999349?accountid=10358.

"Gentrification Displaces Oakland Residents." *University Wire,* Sep 22, 2017.
http://proxy.lib.csus.edu/login?url=https://search-proquest-
com.proxy.lib.csus.edu/docview/1941480098?accountid=10358.

"Staff Editorial: Bay Area Gentrification." *University Wire,* Apr 04, 2014.
   http://proxy.lib.csus.edu/login?url=https://search-proquest-
   com.proxy.lib.csus.edu/docview/1672199945?accountid=10358.

Arnold, Eric K. "Oakland Gang Injunctions: Gentrification or Public Safety?" *Race, Poverty
   & the Environment* 18, no. 2 (2011): 70-74. http://www.jstor.org/stable/41554793.

Bayliss, Deborah. "Blacks and the Elusive Attainment of Economic Power." *Chicago
   Citizen,* May 14, 2014. http://proxy.lib.csus.edu/login?url=https://search-
   proquest-com.proxy.lib.csus.edu/docview/1531098343?accountid=10358.

Brown, Elaine. "Stop the Whitewashing of Oakland District 3." *Oakland Post,* Nov 17,
   1999. http://proxy.lib.csus.edu/login?url=https://search-proquest-
   com.proxy.lib.csus.edu/docview/367091896?accountid=10358.

Elinson, Zusha. "As Mayor, Brown Remade Oakland's Downtown and Himself." The
   New York Times. September 02, 2010.
   http://www.nytimes.com/2010/09/03/us/politics/03bcbrown.html.

Epstein, Ken A. "Oakland Rents Rise Astronomically, Long-Time Home Owners Face
   Foreclosure." *Oakland Post,* Oct, 2013.
   http://proxy.lib.csus.edu/login?url=https://search-proquest-
   com.proxy.lib.csus.edu/docview/1463076158?accountid=10358.

Self, Robert. "'To Plan Our Liberation'." *Journal of Urban History* 26, no. 6 (2000): 759-92.
   doi:10.1177/009614420002600603.

Sheldon, Jessica. "Going Uptown in Downtown Oakland: Market-Rate Housing as a
   Redevelopment Tool." *APA's Economic Development Division Graduate Scholarship,*
   February 6, 2009. https://planning-org-uploaded
   media.s3.amazonaws.com/legacy_resources/divisions/economic/scholarships/20
   09/pdf/sheldon.pdf.

Whelan, Robbie. "The New Urban Pioneers: Companies Spruce Up Neighborhoods,
   Putting Gentrification in Overdrive." *Wall Street Journal,* Aug 14, 2013, Eastern
   edition. http://proxy.lib.csus.edu/login?url=https://search-proquest-
   com.proxy.lib.csus.edu/docview/1420094017?accountid=10358.

The Neocolonial Ramifications of Structural Adjustment and Neoliberalism

Intro

Africa's economic dependency and underdevelopment is rooted in the continent's relationship with European dominance upon colonization. During colonization, European interests governed the regulation and development of commodity markets in Africa.[44] The main feature of this colonial trade relationship was the export of primary commodities to Europe, curating the dependency relationship prior to independence.[45] The current debt crisis, and strife of monocrop commodity markets are colonial inheritances which have been impediments to the growth of African economies. Western influences on the continent post-colonization have been attempts to absolve its colonial economic propensities. Those attempts proved to be counterintuitive, as it made conditions worse for African nations. The proliferation of Neoliberal ideals and the augmentation of Structural Adjustment Programs exacerbated economic conditions on the continent; it deepened the continent's dependency on western market characteristics, precipitously increased the amount of external debt African nations amassed and made the continent extremely vulnerable to influxes of commodity prices. Between the years of 1974 and 2000, debt in Sub-Saharan Africa grew from $11b to $223.3b.[46] This massive debt accumulation perpetuated the underdevelopment of African economies. African nations began to prioritize payments on external debt, which could've been used to develop various sectors within the African economy. The extent as to how external influences, and more explicitly external debt aggrandizes African dependency on the west can be

---

[44] Alemayehu Geda Fole. "The Historical Origin of African Debt Crisis." p.72
[45] Ibid…,
[46] Ibid…, p.61

summarized by Kwame Nkrumah. In which he contends: "The essence of neocolonialism is that the State which is subject to it is, in theory, independent and has all the trappings of international sovereignty. In reality its economic system and thus its political system is directed from outside."[47] This paper will analyze the role of colonialism on the African economy and external debt, as well as the exacerbation of external debt upon the introduction of Neoliberal ideals and Structural Adjustment, and lastly how these propensities affected Civil Society.

Historic Analysis

European expansion to, and colonization of, Africa must be seen as an attempt to acquire political power, via colonization, that would be commensurate with, and further consolidate, its economic power at home.[48] The Berlin Conference marked the proliferation of European expansion, and subsequent scramble for Africa. However, the emergence of the Atlantic Slave Trade prior to the Berlin Conference marks the bourgeoning of the dependency relationship as Africa's role largely becomes the supplier of slave labor to American Plantations.[49] During this period, African autonomy begins to be subverted by western influences; its economy would also begin to be shaped by foreign requirements.[50] African nations came into the periphery as European states engaged in Trans-Atlantic trade with the purpose of aggrandizing metropole economies. European expansion was focused on using expropriated value from slave and coerced labor to incorporate new areas under primary crop production, as well as increasing the rate of production of existing primary commodities.[51] The products from the plantations would in

---

[47] Alex Thomson. "An Introduction to African Politics." p.186
[48] Peter P Ekeh. "Colonialism and the Two Publics in Africa: A Theoretical Statement." p.95
[49] Samir Amin, and Cherita Girvan. "Underdevelopment and Dependence in Black Africa — Origins and Contemporary Forms." p.183
[50] Ibid...,
[51] Alemayehu Geda Fole. "The Historical Origin of African Debt Crisis." p.71

return be sold in European markets, constituting a mercantilist trade monopoly.[52] European influence would cause the growth of these commodity markets to reflect metropole interests. As a result, the African economy would develop distinct inclinations. Domestic markets would be underdeveloped because African nations would mainly export raw materials and import manufactured products.[53] Additionally, investment would be focused on developing sectors of the economy for export which were beneficial to metropole interests. Thus, a dependency relationship is cultivated as the colonizing country retains a monopoly over trade with the colonized state and controls the import and exports tendencies of the African economy.

Colonial rule cemented the African economy to the periphery. Metropole economies strengthened practices and institutions which would increase the demand for, and consumption of European manufactured goods, as well increasing the production of the raw materials for export to Europe. Thus, the encroachment of colonial influences on African states inextricably linked the import and export flows to the desires of the European economy.[54] The colonizing economy achieved this dependency through monetization and state regulation.[55] The colonial government repudiated prior African forms of currency and integrated their standards of exchange; currency integration severed many economic ties within state, as the exchange rate value reflected the value of colonial monetary units.[56] Metropole currencies, in return were used to implement a punitive tax system on African groups, ensuring the currency proliferated throughout sectors in the colonized economy.[57] As a result, the colonial unit of exchange was established as the

[52] Samir Amin, and Cherita Girvan. "Underdevelopment and Dependence in Black Africa — Origins and Contemporary Forms." p.183
[53] Alemayehu Geda Fole. "The Historical Origin of African Debt Crisis." p.73
[54] Moses Ochonu. "African Colonial Economies: State Control, Peasant Maneuvers, and Unintended Outcomes." p.8
[55] Ibid...,
[56] Ibid...,
[57] Ibid...,

complete medium of exchange between the colonizer and the colony.[58] Colonialism

ensured the state economy was controlled and regulated by the metropole. The state

heavily regulated the state's commerce in favor of European firms, shippers and produce

buyers.[59] With control over state institutions, the colonial government implemented

practices which isolated farmers from exporting directly, remaining middle men, and

dependent on European credit and control.[60] These colonial economic mechanisms were

used to create a peasantry class of indigenous Africans who produced export products

which were dependent on the supply and demand interests of European markets.

As African nations gained their independence, the economic tendencies from

colonization remained. In fact, the propensities of a commodity export economy

exacerbated dependency on external influences. Emanating from the colonial state, the

independent African state retained control over market operations. This would mean

public spending would be used to maintain African market efficiency. Consequently, this

also places the burden of expanding the commodity market on the State government. To

that end, external debt became ubiquitous to African economies because export earnings

weren't sufficient to finance the level of public spending, which was required for its

maintenance and expansion.[61] International market volatility would also have pervasive

effects on the external debt needs for the African economy. The prices for commodities

produced in Africa precipitously dropped on the international market which led to

increased loans from bilateral and multilateral creditors; granted from the Paris and

London Clubs.[62] Data from the World Bank in 2001 highlights that the debt to export and

---

[58] Moses Ochonu. "African Colonial Economies: State Control, Peasant Maneuvers, and Unintended Outcomes." p.8
[59] Ibid…, p.9
[60] Moses Ochonu. "African Colonial Economies: State Control, Peasant Maneuvers, and Unintended Outcomes." p.9
[61] Alemayehu Geda Fole. "The Historical Origin of African Debt Crisis." p.73
[62] Ibid…, p.68

debt to GNP ratio for Africa rose from 100 and 24 percent in 1971-1974 to 142 and 108 in 1995-1999.[63] Structural Adjustment Plans were the IMF's response to ballooning African Debt. The IMF believed liberalizing trade and finance, raising domestic interest rates, as well as reducing public spending, and privatizing State Owned Enterprises would absolve the efficiency problems in the African economy. However, this neoliberal concept would prove to be detrimental to economies in Africa; as it has a role in the aforementioned debt to export ratio. According to the IMF, during adjustment programs, it is likely that all components of absorption will decline: cuts in government expenditures and the contradictory effects of those cuts will decrease both public and private consumption and investment, whereas increased interest rates will independently discourage investments...[64]; dilapidating the business climate neoliberalism is intended to create. A World Bank study suggests that adjustment program reduce real levels of consumption as well reducing of exchange rates, which results in decreased imports.[65] To this end, with most African governments relying heavily on government intervention in markets to run the economy, and development being impeded by quasi-colonial policies, the implementation of Structural Adjustment Programs subverted the state's legitimacy and inadvertently would bolster an informal economy.

External Influences on Domestic Markets

Colonial bearings on African export economies caused nations to be heavily susceptible to international market volatility. The Arab oil boycott in 1973 – 1974 would have adverse effects on oil importing countries in Africa. The boycott caused the price of oil per barrel to increase exponentially. The Federal Reserve cites the oil shortage would

---

[63] Alemayehu Geda Fole. "The Historical Origin of African Debt Crisis." p.68
[64] Ramón E. López, and Vinod Thomas. "Import Dependency and Structural Adjustment in Sub-Saharan Africa." p.197
[65] Ibid…, p.198

cause the price of oil to increase from $2.90 per barrel before the embargo to $11.65 per

barrel in January 1974.[66] This impact of world inflation is especially detrimental to less

developed countries, as highlighted previously it aids in their underdevelopment.

Additionally, a second oil shock in 1979 would also create turmoil in international markets.

The Iranian revolution precipitated a decrease in OPEC oil supply, drastically raising prices

in the international market. The resulting effect was a spike in oil prices from $13 per

barrel in 1979 to $34 per barrel in 1980.[67] At the same time, African nations were still

besieged to colonial ties of primary commodity and cash crop export as well as the

mailability of external trade.[68] (African Crisis, 1082). The Agriculture sector was also

susceptible to changes in international market linkages. As the prices for industrial, and

manufactured import goods increased, the prices for non-petroleum export commodities

decreased, consuming most of African nation's net foreign exchange which wasn't used to

pay back foreign debt.[69]

The acceptance of structural adjustment plans to help finance the state ran

economy would yield disparaging results on African nations upon the spike in domestic

interest rates by the Federal Reserve in the United States. During turmoil throughout the

1970's the IMF stepped in to assist the capital flows of African economies, making them

even more dependent on external flows to help run the domestic economy. However, IMF

loans were accompanied with neoliberal conditionality which opened the country to

asymmetric trade relations within the international market. Structural adjustment packages

include trade liberalization, currency devaluation, the removal of government subsidies and

[66] Michael Corbett. "Oil Shock of 1973–74."
[67] Samantha Gross "What Iran's 1979 Revolution Meant for US and Global Oil Markets."
[68] Jackson, Henry F. "The African Crisis: Drought and Debt." p.1082
[69] Ibid…, p.1085

price controls, "cost recovery" in health and education… and increased interest rates.[70] As mentioned earlier, the characteristics of external debt was to bilateral and multilateral creditors. Under structural adjustment, the IMF became the largest creditor of African debt. The ability for African nations to repay their debt would become insurmountable as Paul Volker, then chairman of the Federal Reserve, would raise domestic interest rates to 20 percent in 1980. Consequently, debt servicing has been a large impediment to African nation development. The IMF defines debit service as:

> The debt-to-exports ratio is defined as the ratio of total outstanding debt at the end of the year to the economy's exports of goods and services for any one year. This ratio can be used as a measure of sustainability because an increasing debt-to-exports ratio over time, for a given interest rate, implies that total debt is growing faster than the economy's basic source of external income, indicating that the country may have problems meeting its debt obligations in the future[71]

The beginning of the 1980s saw African debt service ratio reach an average of 30 – 40 percent. At the time, the IMF and World Bank considered a country to have a sustainability problem if more than 20 percent of a nation's net export went to servicing its debt obligations.[72] Debt servicing has been instrumental in the perpetuation of African nation underdevelopment and status in the periphery. Servicing foreign debt erodes the ability for nations to grow their foreign exchange reserve, which is made available for imports.[73] The debt stock also denigrates the business climate needed to attract investment, while reducing the confidence of domestic investors as well.[74] Lastly, because of the pressure created to repay foreign debt, physical and social infrastructures become dilapidated, stemming from a lack of investment.[75] As mentioned above, the IMF contends that all levels of consumption will decrease under structural adjustment; structural

---

[70] D.E. Logie, and J. Woodroffe. "Structural Adjustment: The Wrong Prescription for Africa?" p.42
[71] "External Debt Statistics. Guide for Compilers and Users."
[72] Jackson, Henry F. "The African Crisis: Drought and Debt." p.1086
[73] Alemayehu Geda Fole. "The Historical Origin of African Debt Crisis." p.68
[74] Ibid…,
[75] Ibid…,

adjustment subsequently discourages both domestic and foreign investment, therefore

perpetuating underdevelopment in African economies where consumption is already

devoid due to colonial propensities.

Structural Adjustment effects on Civil Society

Structural adjustment programs seek to remove the state from market operations. The "cost recovery" associated with these plans is rhetoric which justifies cuts in public expenditure to public services such as health and education. Prior to structural adjustment, the population with a primary education doubled from 36 percent, to 79 percent in 1980.[76] Upon the introduction of adjustment programs, medical and educational fees were augmented to pay for the services as they were no longer subsidized by the state.[77] Simultaneously, since the state was the largest employer of its citizens, structural adjustment caused wages to fall and unemployment to rise[78]. As a result of a structural adjustment program in Zimbabwe in 1991, the poor could no longer afford access to health care. Implementation of program resulted in a decrease in health expenditure by 20 percent, and education by 14 percent.[79] Effects of structural adjustment have also been disproportional to women and children: the removal of subsidies on food, has led to inadequate nutrition, which also affects women during pregnancy.[80] Cuts in health care access, results in inadequate family planning, and increased deaths during child birth.[81] High unemployment rates lead to a male dominated workforce, marginalizing women to the periphery of the labor pool.[82] The execution of educational fees displaces young women in schools at a higher rate than young men.[83] To address these socioeconomic conditions created by neoliberal economics, International Finance Institutions began to

---

[76] D.E. Logie, and J. Woodroffe. "Structural Adjustment: The Wrong Prescription for Africa?" p.41
[77] Ibid..., p.42
[78] Ibid...,
[79] Ibid...,
[80] Ibid...,
[81] Ibid...,
[82] Ibid...,
[83] Ibid...,

implement poverty alleviation programs into adjustment programs, however the repercussions were already prolific.[84] Moreover, the degradational effects of structural adjustment would cause Non-Governmental Organizations (NGOs) to be aggrandized with civil society. NGO's were perceived as important actors because they could circumvent the bureaucracy of the state while correcting failures in the market.[85] Albeit the strides made to improve socioeconomic conditions of the poor, when compared to the performance of other aid programs, NGOs fell short.[86] It has been observed that NGOs fall short because of their inability to reach beyond a micro-scale focus, and ineffectiveness of ensuring long-term institutional sustainability.[87] (413). Because NGOs are peripheral to the systems they are trying to change and lack the leverage necessary to maintain their influence when there are other, more powerful interests at work.[88] To this end, structural adjustment programs have been egregious to the development of the African economy, while taking civil society and the poor as collateral, pushing them to the periphery of an already peripheral economy.

Conclusion

Africa's condition as a peripheral, dependent economy, consumed with external debt is a direct result of the market propensities inherited from colonialism. External influences dictating the direction of African markets would deepen the dependency relationship between the core nations and the peripheral African continent. The creation of a primary good – export economy, resulted in the abrasive relationship which would push the African economy further into the periphery. The ostensible attempts by Western

---

[84] Alex Thomson. "An Introduction to African Politics." p.195
[85] Henrik Secher Marcussen. "NGOs, the State and Civil Society." p.407
[86] Ibid…, p.412
[87] Ibid…, p.413
[88] Ibid…, p.413

influences to absolve these economic problems had detrimental effects on the economies of Africa. An IMF report contended that all factors of consumption would decrease upon structural adjustment. Counterintuitively, the IMF perceived austerity, devaluation, finance liberalization, trade liberalization, and cuts in public expenditure as necessary strategies to alleviate the economic problems of Africa, and spur development. Structural Adjustment Programs worsened economic conditions, disproportionately for the poor, the women, and the children. Conclusively, structural programs exacerbated the already fragile African economy.

Bibliography

"External Debt Statistics. Guide for Compilers and Users." 2004. doi:10.1787/9789264065161-en.

Amin, Samir, and Cherita Girvan. "Underdevelopment and Dependence in Black Africa — Origins and Contemporary Forms." *Social and Economic Studies* 22, no. 1 (March 1973): 177-96.

Corbett, Michael. "Oil Shock of 1973–74." Federal Reserve History. Accessed May 06, 2019. https://www.federalreservehistory.org/essays/oil_shock_of_1973_74.

Ekeh, Peter P. "Colonialism and the Two Publics in Africa: A Theoretical Statement." *Comparative Studies in Society and History* 17, no. 1 (January 1975): 91-112. doi:10.4324/9780429502538-7.

Fole, Alemayehu Geda. "The Historical Origin of African Debt Crisis." *Eastern Africa Social Science Research Review* 19, no. 1 (2003): 59-89. doi:10.1353/eas.2002.0012.

Gross, Samantha. "What Iran's 1979 Revolution Meant for US and Global Oil Markets." Brookings. Accessed May 07, 2019. https://www.brookings.edu/blog/order-from-chaos/2019/03/05/what-irans-1979-revolution-meant-for-us-and-global-oil-markets/.

Jackson, Henry F. "The African Crisis: Drought and Debt." *Foreign Affairs* 63, no. 5 (1985): 1081-094. doi:10.2307/20042371.

Logie, D. E., and J. Woodroffe. "Structural Adjustment: The Wrong Prescription for Africa?" *BMJ: British Medial Journal* 307, no. 6895 (1993): 41-44. doi:10.1136/bmj.307.6895.41.

López, Ramón E., and Vinod Thomas. "Import Dependency and Structural Adjustment in Sub-Saharan Africa." *The World Bank Economic Review* 4, no. 2 (1990): 195-207. doi:10.1093/wber/4.2.195.

Marcussen, Henrik Secher. "NGOs, the State and Civil Society." *Review of African Political Economy* 23, no. 69 (September 1996): 405-23. doi:10.1080/03056249608704205.

Ochonu, Moses. "African Colonial Economies: State Control, Peasant Maneuvers, and Unintended Outcomes." *History Compass* 11, no. 1 (2013): 1-13. doi:10.1111/hic3.12024.

Thomson, Alex. "An Introduction to African Politics." 2005. doi:10.4324/9780203403150.

Contemporary Neocolonialism of Africa by the United States and China

Africa's subservience has a direct correlation between the continent's historic subjugation as well as its contemporary exploitation. Historically, the continent of Africa has been subject to colonization and economic decimation by northern powers. Prior to decolonization, hard power has been the primary means of coercion to establish dominance over the continent. Contemporarily, the utilization of debt has caused nations in Africa to succumb to neocolonialism. Under the guise of economic neoliberalism, the United States and China have both established a stronghold over the domestic economies of African Nations. The United States has proliferated its influence through the amalgamation of economic thought by the US Treasury-World Bank-IMF complex, otherwise known as the Washington Consensus. The utilization of structural adjustment loans to open domestic markets and allow for trade liberalization as well as financial liberalization which expropriates resources back to the north has been the primary means of expanding the United States' power. China's strategy has been to directly invest in the economies of these nations; albeit seeming as an amicable investment, China has displayed its neocolonial motives upon the introduction of Chinese businesses as well the implementation of Chinese citizens within the labor forces of African nations. This essay will analyze how both superpowers have exploited African nations and perpetuated subjugation by employing ideals of economic neoliberalism.

The US Treasury-World Bank-IMF complex has accepted the ideology of economic neoliberalism not only as being beneficial to developing countries, but imperative to achieve economic stability. With the United States exerting its influence over these monetary institutions, it has been able to leverage its position, extending its influence, and ultimately its dominance. The Washington Consensus has been able to propagate and maintain its dominance by exploiting the instability of African nations following decolonization. African nations who needed monetary assistance to continue developmental programs were granted structural adjustment loans from the IMF which imposed conditionality measures on them. "IMF conditionality ensures that borrowers agree to adopt specific economic policy in return for IMF loans, and the conditions become more stringent as a member borrows more from the IMF in relation to its quota."[89] This conditionality forces African nations to accept economic neoliberalism; imposing its tenets: austerity, trade liberalization, finance liberalization, and privatization. Under the guise of being imperative and beneficial to developing nations, this neoliberal reconstruction of economies has allowed for the United States to pillage economies and allow for private corporations to establish control over the host state's economy. Contrarily, many loan recipients argue that structural adjustment loans do little to benefit their economic growth, additionally it erodes their borders and degrades their sovereignty.[90]

The argument against economic neoliberal being beneficial to developing nations can be refuted by emphasizing the failures of structural adjustment to aid in the development of African nations. In article by Robin Broad titled *Development: The Market is Not Enough,* the dialectic arguing against economic neoliberalism's benefits is conveyed. Focusing on the social and economic degradation that occurs under the guild of a neoliberal market, the author contends that structural adjustment increases squalor among the poor population. As the need for exports increases to make loan payments, the unsustainable exploitation of natural resources proliferates throughout developing

---

[89] Theodore Cohn. *Global Political Economy.* p.143
[90] Ibid…,

nations.[91] Furthermore, the austerity measures imposed as a result of the conditionality of the structural adjustment loan seeks to reduce government spending in order to ensure the balance of payment transactions are equalized. Consequently, this causes a drastic cutback in social programs.[92] Citing the World Bank which concluded that the implementation of structural adjustment is complimented with "sharply deteriorating social indicators… in which people below the poverty line will probably suffer irreparable damage on health, nutrition, and education."[93] Structural adjustment in Africa has especially proven to have negatives effects on domestic economies. A study conducted by the United Nations Economic Commission for Africa cited a report from the World Bank, which concluded that after the implementation of structural adjustment programs, 15 African nations were worse off in a number of economic categories.[94]

In an attempt to challenge the economic neoliberal regime, leaders and representatives of diverse social movements, political organizations, and debt coalitions from 35 countries in Africa, as well as additional nations within the global south met in 1999 to overcome the debt-related domination by the Global North over the Global South.[95] Calling for the repudiation and eradication of the economic institutional ideology that is responsible for the utilization of debt as means of controlling the economies of the Global South, the leaders of the South-South Summit "forcefully denounce the growing concentration of wealth, power, and resources in the world economy as the essential cause of the increase in violence, impoverishment, and indebtedness'…"[96] Leaders of the South-South Summit uphold that the debt accrued by nations in the Global South is an

---

[91] Robin Broad, John Cavanagh, and Walden Bello. "Development: The Market Is Not Enough."
[92] Ibid…,
[93] Robin Broad, John Cavanagh, and Walden Bello. "Development: The Market Is Not Enough."
[94] Ibid…,
[95] Robin Broad. *Global Backlash: Citizen Initiatives for a Just World Economy.* p.275
[96] Ibid…, p.276

ideological and political tool in which the main actor for its proliferation is the IMF and its

structural programs. Reverberating the effects of colonialism which have transcended and

allowed for the contemporary exploitative climate the leaders contend: "the accumulation

of Foreign Debt in countries of the South is a product of the crisis of that very same

system and it is used to perpetuate the plunder and domination of our nations often with

the acquiescence, if not active collaboration, of local elites."[97] Thus, a display of how

Africa and nations in the Global South have transitioned from colonialism to

neocolonialism with the accumulation of exploitive debt.

Essential to China's neocolonial strategy has been the integration of finance and

the acceptance of inward foreign direct investment by African nations. "Foreign direct

investment is capital investment in physical or tangible assets such as a branch plant or

subsidiary of an MNC in which the investor has some operating control."[98] The

liberalization of finance is one of the primary tenets of economic neoliberalism. A

domestic economy which incorporates the ideals of economic neoliberalism will open its

domestic market to foreign direct investment. Therefore, a country who accepts this

economic ideology successively opens its economy to the integration of finance capital and

subsequently the acceptance of the foreign direct investment. Foreign direct investment

can come in two forms. One form is derived from the investment of capital by foreign

banks. The second form is through the direct investment of capital by multinational

corporations.

China has been aggressive with its investment into the economies of African

nations. Following a forum in Beijing with Chinese leader Xi Jinping and representatives

---

[97] Robin Broad. *Global Backlash: Citizen Initiatives for a Just World Economy.* p.276
[98] Theodore Cohn. *Global Political Economy.* p.134

from almost every country in Africa, Jinping pledged infrastructure investments of $60

billion over the next three year with "no political strings attached."[99] This investment

pledge by Jinping makes China the largest creditor to the Sub Saharan African region.[100]

Although this may seem as an amicable investment by the Chinese leader, Chinese

involvement in African nations has demonstrated neocolonial behaviors. In Uganda in

2017, investments from China contributed over 40% of total direct investments, totaling

$290 dollars being invested into Uganda's infrastructure.[101] Thus, making Uganda one of

the top four investment destinations for China in Sub Saharan Africa.[102] Conversely, a

2017 report on Uganda's external debt concluded that the country's total external debt has

amounted to $7.163 billion.[103] Another report demonstrates that in the 2010-2011 fiscal

year Uganda's debt to the International Developmental Association decreased from 61.9%

to 45.2%, however in that same time period Uganda debt to China increased from 3.3% to

20.3%.[104] Indicating an upward trend in indebtedness to China. The Chinese debt trap in

Zambia has already began to unravel its neocolonial characteristics. Zesco, Zambia's

national power utility has been reported as coming under Chinese control as Zambia

continues to default on their loan repayments.[105] Additionally, there have already been

reports concluding that ZNBC, Zambia's national broadcaster is being run by the

Chinese.[106] Ostensibly, seeming to control dissent against Chinese investment, Zambian

officials deported renowned Pan-African, Professor Lumumba prior to his speech in

September regarding "Africa in the age of China's influence and Global Geo-

---

[99] Adam Withnall. "African Leaders Leave Beijing Forum Hailing 'new World Order' as China Offers $60bn Investment."
[100] Witney Schneidman, and Joel Wiegert. "Competing in Africa: China, the European Union, and the United States."
[101] Pascal Kwesiga, Taddeo Bwambale, and Apollo Mubiru. "More Chinese Companies Moving to Africa."
[102] Ibid...,
[103] "Uganda External Debt." Zambia GDP - per Capita (PPP) – Economy.
[104] Kafeero, Stephen. "Uganda Needs 94 Years to Clear Debt."
[105] Takudzwa Chiwanza. "China To Take Over Zambia's National Power Utility ZESCO - How Zambia Is Becoming Chinese Property."
[106] Ibid...,

Dynamics."[107] Therefore, China's reign over the Sub Saharan region of Africa demonstrates the exploitative characteristics of economic neoliberalism perpetuating colonialism through means of the usurpation of debt.

The application of economic neoliberal ideals by both the United States and China has led to African nations becoming stuck in a debt trap in which they cannot rid themselves of. Although the means by which the debt is accrued is different, the result, nevertheless remains the same. The augmentation of debt through structural adjustment programs through the IMF has proven to dilapidate living standards as opposed to eradicating poverty. Complimenting economic squalor is the indebtedness in which the country as whole is also consumed by, thus succumbing to the agenda of the US Treasury-World Bank-IMF complex. China's foreign direct investment merely reallocates debt from one monetary institution to the Chinese government. Although seeming to be benevolent, the investment from the China is in fact exploitative, catching African nations in a debt trap. Hence, a demonstration of how Africa is being recolonized under the guise of economic neoliberalism by both the United States and Africa.

---

[107] Sebastiane Ebatamehi. "Zambia Deported Renowned Pan-African, Prof. PLO Lumumba, for Speaking Up Against China."

Bibliography

"Uganda External Debt." Zambia GDP - per Capita (PPP) - Economy. January 20, 2018.
Accessed December 02, 2018.
https://www.indexmundi.com/uganda/debt_external.html.

Broad, Robin, John Cavanagh, and Walden Bello. "Development: The Market Is Not
Enough." Foreign Policy, no. 81 (1990): 144. doi:10.2307/1148813.

Broad, Robin. Global Backlash: Citizen Initiatives for a Just World Economy. Lanham,
MD: Rowman & Littlefield, 2002.

Chiwanza, Takudzwa Hillary. "China To Take Over Zambia's National Power Utility
ZESCO - How Zambia Is Becoming Chinese Property." The African Exponent.
September 10, 2018. Accessed December 02, 2018.
https://www.africanexponent.com/post/9124-zambia-is-slowly-becoming-
chinese-property-due-to-accumulating-debts.

Cohn, Theodore. *Global Political Economy.* New York, NY: Routledge, 2016.

Ebatamehi, Sebastiane. "Zambia Deported Renowned Pan-African, Prof. PLO Lumumba,
for Speaking Up Against China." The African Exponent. September 29, 2018.
Accessed December 02, 2018. https://www.africanexponent.com/post/9177-
kenyas-professor-patrick-lumumba-denied-entry-into-zambia-deported-back-to-
kenya

Kafeero, Stephen. "Uganda Needs 94 Years to Clear Debt." Daily Monitor. April 07, 2018.
Accessed December 02, 2018.
https://www.monitor.co.ug/News/National/Uganda-needs-94-years-clear-debt--
/688334-4375770-nu7qh4z/index.html.

Kwesiga, Pascal, Taddeo Bwambale, and Apollo Mubiru. "More Chinese Companies
Moving to Africa." Www.newvision.co.ug. August 16, 2018. Accessed December
02, 2018. https://www.newvision.co.ug/new_vision/news/1483743/chinese-
companies-moving-africa.

Schneidman, Witney, and Joel Wiegert. "Competing in Africa: China, the European Union,
and the United States." Brookings.edu. April 18, 2018. Accessed December 02,
2018. https://www.brookings.edu/blog/africa-in-focus/2018/04/16/competing-
in-africa-china-the-european-union-and-the-united-states/.

Withnall, Adam. "African Leaders Leave Beijing Forum Hailing 'new World Order' as
China Offers $60bn Investment." The Independent. September 04, 2018. Accessed
December 02, 2018. https://www.independent.co.uk/news/world/asia/china-
africa-bejing-forum-investment-interest-free-loans-a8522376.html.

Colonial and Neocolonial Idioms of Black Inferiority

The subordination of Black life by those sworn to uphold colonial law and order has been endemic prior the inception of the Slave Patrol. The asymmetric social and economic relationship between the white and Black race is embedded in the United States Constitution; it has been maintained by legal statute and enforced by institutions of law enforcement. The contentions between the Black community and the police are derived from the oppressive relationship between the slave and the slave catcher. The justification for the inception of this relationship emanates from the colonial and imperial ideologies of Black mental, and civil inferiority. European colonizers justified chattel slavery under the presumption of Africans being less civilized, less intellectual, and therefore subhuman. The result of this ideology led to slaves being utilized and exploited as property under the guise of the United States Constitution. To protect the interests of the Planter class, the slave patrol was conceived to return runaway slaves to plantation owners in order to resume their marginal rate of profit. This dehumanization of Black lives has perpetuated upon the signing of the emancipation proclamation. The institution of law enforcement has been instrumental to this reification of Black subordination, socially and economically. The burgeoning of the War on Crime exacerbated the dichotomy as well; increasing police surveillance in Black neighborhoods successively led to the incarceration *en mass* as well as disproportional killings of Black individuals. To an extent, the concept of policing has shifted into an entity of revenue generation. Police departments such as that in Ferguson, Missouri have exploited the Black community as means of municipal revenue accumulation, which was also reinforced by the Judicial system. Meanwhile presumably progressive states like California led the nation in police killings of its citizens in 2017. Up until August of 2019, the state's penal code regarding police use of force had not been amended since 1872, nine years after the signing of the emancipation proclamation; in which after its promulgation, Black people were still perceived as subhuman. To this end, there is an unequivocal correlation between the imperial and colonial ideologies of Black inferiority and dehumanization during the antebellum period of the United States and its precipitation to the contemporary marginalization by public officials, legal statute, and law enforcement.

In order to precipitate their colonial rule, European colonizers had to persuade their citizens as well as the colonized nations as being benign in their encroachment of power. These practices can be identified as imperial and colonial ideologies of legitimation. Imperial ideologies of legitimation seek to justify imperial expansion as being beneficial to all colonizing nations and every taxpayer in them. Conversely, Europeans used colonial ideologies of legitimation to explain to Africans why being colonized was beneficial to them. Accompanied by Missionaries, European colonizers asserted that the African past was backwards, contending that their ancestor-spiritual worship was evil, and needed to be repudiated. They forced Africans to accept Western ideologies as well as Christianity, under the guise of saving them from their past. Former Prime Minister and President of Kenya, Jomo Kenyatta remarks "when the missionaries arrived, the Africans had the land and the missionaries had the Bible. They taught us how to pray with our eyes closed. When we opened them, they had the land and we had the Bible." The manipulation of biblical scriptures was instrumental in reinforcing the subordination of Black people globally.

Subverted within these colonial ideological tactics was the permeation and proliferation of Black intellectual inferiority. The augmentation of scientific racism helped espouse the ideology of Black inferiority, and successively a justification for slavery. The belief in the eternal malingering of slaves was one tenant of scientific racism[108]. Throughout epochs, Europeans have perceived African men as uncivilized, and overly aggressive. Findings as early as 160 A.D. highlight Roman physician Galen who described African men as possessing oversized sexual organs and inferior intelligence.[109] During the seventeenth and eighteenth century, justifications for slavery and theories of scientific racism were substantiated through the Bible as well as science.[110] As a result, the dichotomy between monogenists and polygenists promulgated. Monogenists believed both the white and Black race share a common ancestral ape and a single species. Conversely, polygenists presented the antithesis in which the two races derive from different ancestral alignments. More purportedly, according to polygenists, Blacks were physically inferior and were malingerers, hypersexual, and indolent. In the early years of the eighteenth century, Blacks were most often compared to beasts… This presumption of Black indolence and lack of adult judgement rendered them unable to care for themselves and gave another justification for slavery.[111] Examining the journals from medical scientists such as Josiah Clark Nott, this notion has been substantiated as Nott extends the justification for slavery beyond medial research to biblical references. Nott deduced Blacks as children of Ham, son of Noah, who, along with his progeny, was "marked" and condemned to be servant to his brothers for having viewed his father's nakedness.[112] Additionally, Nott insisted that yellow fever and malaria were visited upon whites as divine punishment for not enslaving Blacks. Contending that non-whites contracted these diseases as a result of usurping the "natural" Black role as laborers in the fields.[113] Under the premise of white supremacy in every field of human endeavor, the dehumanization of the Black race was accepted and proliferated as a justification for their subservience. This perception would last throughout the antebellum era of the United States while also serving as contemporary justifications for the dehumanization of Black lives.

To further understand the relationship between the slave and slave patrol, the utilization of the slave as a financial instrument must be analyzed. To that end, the importance of cotton to the economy of the United States' south must also be contextualized. Although the Constitution of the United States was signed in 1787, profit earnings off slave labor had already been utilized. According to Sven Beckert in the *Empire of Cotton*, cotton as a commodity became a very lucrative not only domestically, but internationally as well. The southern region particularly made exponential profits within the cotton market because of the exploitation of slave labor and the amount of arable land that was accessible. In 1786 the United States began to recognize the lucrative potential of cotton with the conception of mechanized cotton textile production in the United Kingdom.[114] This would cause the rapid expansion of the domestic cotton market to rely on more slaves to extend its profit. In fact, the states of Georgia and North

---

[108]Harriet A. Washington. *Medical Apartheid The Dark History of Medical Experimentation on Black Americans from Colonial Times to the Present.* p.32
[109] Ibid…, p.34
[110] Ibid…, p.34
[111] Ibid…, p.35
[112] Ibid…, p.39
[113] Ibid…, p.39-40
[114] Sven Beckert. *Empire of Cotton: A New History of Global Capitalism.* London: Penguin Books, 2015. p.10

Carolina in the 1790s saw a dramatic increase in their slave population. In Georgia during the 1790s, the slave population nearly doubled, to sixty thousand. Over twenty years in North Carolina, the slave population increased from twenty-one thousand in 1970 to seventy thousand.[115] The reification of lower-class status of Black slaves emanates from their utilization as property and financial instruments. Additionally, the economic utilization of slaves came in the form of collateral or property to be loaned. Beckert highlights "since the expansion of the cotton agriculture depended on the advance of credit, sometimes secured by mortgages on slaves, most of which derived from the London money market, its patterns now followed the competitive logic of markets rather than the whimsy of regional circumstance…".[116] Moreover, chattel slavery was pertinent to capital investment flows into the United States. In 1843 the American Chamber of Commerce in Liverpool lobbied against the Slave Act; they feared the extension of the Slave act of 1824 in 1843 would "make all mortgages [secured by slaves] and other Securities made… to accomplish any object or contract in relation to any object" unlawful.[117] Thus, a display of the aggrandization of Black lower-class status being exploited for profit. Beckert reifies "It was on the back of cotton, and thus on the backs of slaves, that the United States' economy ascended into the world."[118] This relationship would only precipitate the economic suppression of the Black community post-emancipation.

The premise of slaves being subhuman ostensibly justified through scientific racism and biblical scriptures, as well as their utilization as financial instruments established their status as property within the colonial economy. Therefore, embedded in the constitution of the United States was language intended to preserve the economic structure of colonial subjugation. Article IV, section 2 of the United States at the time read:

> *No Person held to Service or Labour in one State, under the Laws thereof, escaping into another, shall, in Consequence of any Law or Regulation therein, be discharged from such Service or Labour, But shall be delivered up on Claim of the Party to whom such Service or Labour may be due.[119]*

Additionally, the passage of the Fugitive Slave Act by Congress in 1793 would reify the premise of enslaved Africans as property; language of the Fugitive Slave Law of 1793 reads:

> *…[And] it is further agreed between the parties aforesaid, that neither shall entertain, or give countenance to, the enemies of the other, or protect, in their respective states, criminal fugitives, servants, or slaves, but the same to apprehend and secure, and deliver to the state or states, to which such enemies, criminals, servants, or slaves, respectively below.[120]*

The importance of slave labor to the global cotton market which emanated primarily from cotton exports of the United States south has been analyzed in the above text. To this end, the expansion of the 1792 Fugitive Slave Act in the 1850 Compromise

---

[115] Sven Beckert. *Empire of Cotton: A New History of Global Capitalism.* London: Penguin Books, 2015. p.103
[116] Sven Beckert. *Empire of Cotton: A New History of Global Capitalism.* London: Penguin Books, 2015. p.116-117
[117] Ibid…, p.223
[118] Ibid…, p.119
[119] U.S. Const. art. IV, § 2. (This clause is superseded by the 13th Amendment).
[120] *Digital History.*

can be perceived as an expansion in the interests of maintaining the economic mechanisms of the south. Sections 8 and 9 of the Fugitive Slave Act of 1850 incentivized slave catchers to catch and return slaves to their claimants.

> *Section 8: [And] be it further enacted, That the marshals, their deputies, and the clerks of the said District and Territorial Courts, shall be paid, for their services, the like fees as may be allowed for similar services in other cases; and where such services are rendered exclusively in the arrest, custody, and delivery of the fugitive to the claimant, his or her agent or attorney, or where such supposed fugitive may be discharged out of custody for the want of sufficient proof as aforesaid, then such fees are to be paid in whole by such claimant, his or her agent or attorney; and in all cases where the proceedings are before a commissioner, he shall be entitled to a fee of ten dollars in full for his services in each case, upon the delivery of the said certificate to the claimant, his agent or attorney; or a fee of five dollars in cases where the proof shall not, in the opinion of such commissioner, warrant such certificate and delivery, inclusive of all services incident to such arrest and examination, to be paid, in either case, by the claimant, his or her agent or attorney.[121]*

> *Section 9: [And] be it further enacted, That, upon affidavit made by the claimant of such fugitive, his agent or attorney, after such certificate has been issued, that he has reason to apprehend that such fugitive will be rescued by force from his or their possession before he can be taken beyond the limits of the State in which the arrest is made, it shall be the duty of the officer making the arrest to retain such fugitive in his custody, and to remove him to the State whence he fled, and there to deliver him to said claimant, his agent, or attorney. And to this end, the officer aforesaid is hereby authorized and required to employ so many persons as he may deem necessary to overcome such force, and to retain them in his service so long as circumstances may require. The said officer and his assistants, while so employed, to receive the same compensation, and to be allowed the same expenses, as are now allowed by law for transportation of criminals, to be certified by the judge of the district within which the arrest is made, and paid out of the treasury of the United States.[122]*

The relationship between the slave catcher and the enslaved are congenial to the interests of the southern plantation owner. Burgeoning an entity which would be used to maintain the subordination of enslaved Africans as property to a class of white property owners. As underground railroad routes proliferated throughout the south, the global market share of southern cotton would diminish, resulting in the decrease in the rate of profit for owners of surplus labor value – the planter class. As a result, slave catchers (which would materialize into police forces) would become tools for the wealthy to retain and maintain their wealth. Furthermore, the contentions between the enslaved and the slave catchers would not diminish but exacerbate. These propensities can be observed contemporarily as there are many parallels between the subordinate economic status of Black people and their relation to law enforcement, public officials, and legal statute to the interaction of enslaved Africans to the aforementioned entities.

President Franklin Delano Roosevelt was responsible for the inception of New Deal Reform programs which helped bring the country out economic turmoil under the premise of Keynesian economic thought. Keynesian economic thought theorizes that government intervention in the market would allow for the greatest marginal utility among the people, while also promoting domestic economic stability, and full employment. Under President Roosevelt the Federal Housing Administration was conceived in 1934. Through this, government subsidized mortgage packages were created to aid in the proliferation of

---

[121] *Avalon Project - Fugitive Slave Act 1850.*
[122] *Avalon Project - Fugitive Slave Act 1850.*

home ownership; a process called suburbanization in political science discourse. Black people during this time period were isolated from upward economic mobility. Through means of *de jure* and *de facto* economic practices, Black households were isolated from attaining government subsidized mortgages. The underwriting manual of the Federal Housing Administration imposed a number of "economic" ordinances which had racial undertones and reinforced segregation. An interview done by Terry Gross from *National Public Radio* and Richard Rothstein, author of *The Color of Law* illustrates how the FHA underwriting manual subverted the economic bearings of the Black community: "the most important role of the Federal Housing Administration was it subsidized mass-production builders of entire subdivisions, entire suburbs. And it did so with a requirement that no homes be sold to African-Americans and that every home in these subdivisions had a clause in the deed that prohibited resale to African-Americans." To this end, a report taken using statistics from the *1989 Survey of Consumer Finances* highlighted for "most middle-class families, wealth is closely tied to the value of their homes."[123] It is because of policies of this nature, accompanied by redlining, and predatory installment loans that the Black community saw capital leave its neighborhoods, and essentially became underdeveloped. Furthermore, the expropriation of Black capital resulted in the dilapidation of housing and living standards, as well as the propagation of poverty. Mehrsa Baradaran in her book *The Color of Money* asserts that between 1934 and 1968, 98 percent of FHA loans went to white Americans. Thus, New Deal reform programs engendered a thriving white middle class, while cementing Black ghetto subservience.[124]

In congruence with economic immiseration, the War on Drugs disproportionately denigrated the lives of Black people; deriving from a superiority complex, federal laws were enacted to pretentiously combat drug usage in the United States. Conversely, the laws would subsequently engender the first building blocks of over-policing and the mass incarceration of Black communities.

> *"Reefer makes darkies think they're as good as white men." – "There are 100,000 total marijuana smokers in the U.S., and most are Negroes, Hispanics, Filipinos and entertainers. Their Satanic music, jazz and swing result from marijuana use. This marijuana causes white women to seek sexual relations with Negroes, entertainers and any others."[125] – Harry Anslinger*

Rhetoric espoused by Harry Anslinger utilized the inferiority complex placed on Black people which was used to justify enslaving Africans. Anslinger was Commissioner of the U.S. Treasury Department Bureau of Narcotics from 1930 to 1962, chief U.S. delegate to international drug agencies until 1970, and a leading proponent of repressive antidrug measures in the United States.[126] The burgeoning of marijuana prohibition would allow for government regulation of marijuana sales and transport. The laws propagated during this time period would also implement an arduous tax system, as well establish many barriers for entry, ostracizing those without mountains of capital to enter the market. The passage of the Marijuana Tax Act in 1937 allowed for federal regulation and therefore criminalization of the illegal marijuana market. The Boggs Act of 1951 and The Daniel Act

---

[123] Edward Wolff. "How the Pie Is Sliced: America's Growing Concentration of Wealth."
[124] Mehrsa Baradaran. *The Color of Money: Black Banks and the Racial Wealth Gap.*
[125] Laura Smith. "How a Racist Hate-monger Masterminded America's War on Drugs."
[126] "Anslinger, Harry Jacob, and U.S. Drug Policy."

in 1956 would amend and drastically strengthen punitive actions regarding illegal marijuana in the United States.

Boggs Act 1951:

> *SEC. 2. Section 2557 (b) (1) of the Internal Revenue Code is amended to read as follows: "(1) Whoever commits an offense or conspires to commit an offense described in this subchapter, subchapter C of this chapter, or parts V or VI of subchapter A of chapter 27, for which no specific penalty is otherwise provided, shall be fined not more than $2,000 and imprisoned not less than two or more than five years. For a second offense, the offender shall be fined not more than $2,000 and imprisoned not less than five or more than ten years. For a third or subsequent offense, the offender shall be fined not more than $2,000 and imprisoned not less than ten or more than twenty years.*[127]

Daniel Act 1956:

> *SEC. 7237. VIOLATION OF LAWS RELATING TO NARCOTIC DRUGS AND TO MARIHUANA. "(a) WHERE NO SPECIFIC PENALTY IS OTTIERWISE PROVIDED.— Whoever commits an offense, or conspires to commit an offense, described in part I or part II of subchapter A of chapter 39 for which no specific penalty is otherwise provided, shall be imprisoned not less than 2 or more than 10 years and, in addition, may be fined not more than $20,000. For a second offense, the offender shall be imprisoned not less than 5 or more than 20 years and, in addition, may be fined not more than $20,000. For a third or subsequent offense, the offender shall be imprisoned not less than 10 or more than 40 years and, in addition, may be fined not more than $20,000. " (b) SALE OR OTHER TRANSFER WITHOUT WRITIEN ORDER.— Whoever commits an offense, or conspires to commit an offense, described in section 4705 (a) or section 4742 (a) shall be imprisoned not less than 5 or more than 20 years and, in addition, may be fined not more than $20,000. For a second or subsequent offense, the offender shall be imprisoned not less than 10 or more than 40 years and, in addition, may be fined not more than $20,000. If the offender attained the age of 18 before the offense and— "(1) the offense consisted of the sale, barter, exchange, giving away, or transfer of any narcotic drug or marihuana to a person who had not attained the age of 18 at the time of such offense, or " (2) the offense consisted of a conspiracy to commit an offense described in paragraph (1), the offender shall be imprisoned not less than 10 or more than 40 years and, in addition, may be fined not more than $20,000.*[128]

Harry Anslinger reinforced Black subordination and dehumanization. Delineating jazz as satanic while contending that it derives from marijuana usage was an unequivocal strategy to regulate and criminalize marijuana. This strategy would be a precursor for the more notorious War on Drugs and War on Crime by later United States Presidents. It must also be highlighted that the U.S. Treasury Department Bureau of Narcotics materialized into the Drug Enforcement Agency (DEA), which would become a primary tool of the War on Drugs.

President Richard Nixon perpetuated the War on Drugs within Black communities during his tenure. Under his regime, the Controlled Substances Act was passed. The Controlled Substances Act is the federal statute that regulates the manufacture and distribution of controlled substances such as hallucinogens, narcotics, depressants, and stimulants. The Act categorizes drugs into five classifications or "schedules" based on their

---

[127] H.R. 3490, 82nd Congress (1951–1952)
[128] United States. 1956. *Narcotic control act of 1956.*

potential for abuse, status in international treaties, and any medical benefits they may provide. Generally speaking, drugs included in Schedule 1 are the most strictly regulated, because they are deemed to have no medical value.[129] Marijuana, according to the DEA is classified under schedule 1[130], which means drugs placed within this criterion is heavily regulated, and therefore heavily policed. On June 17th, 1971, president Nixon declared drug abuse as "public enemy number one.[131] However, this precarious rhetoric was a strategy to target anti-war protestors and Black neighborhoods. John Ehrlichman, former domestic policy chief for the Nixon administration maintained "The Nixon campaign in 1968, and the Nixon White House after that, had two enemies: the antiwar left and black people... You understand what I'm saying? We knew we couldn't make it illegal to be either against the war or black, but by getting the public to associate the hippies with marijuana and blacks with heroin. And then criminalizing both heavily, we could disrupt those communities... We could arrest their leaders. raid their homes, break up their meetings, and vilify them night after night on the evening news. Did we know we were lying about the drugs? Of course we did."[132] In the following year, Nixon established the Office of Drug Abuse Law Enforcement (ODALE) which would be consolidated and amalgamated with other federal drug agencies, successively creating the DEA, and giving the entity hegemonic control over all aspects of the War on Drugs.

The Black community would soon face further vicissitudes as the Reagan administration would also champion the War on Drugs. On October 14th, 1982 President Ronald Reagan declared illicit drugs to be a threat to national security.[133] Reagan's dogmatic zero tolerance rhetoric not only bolstered police surveillance in Black neighborhoods, but it engendered the militarization of police departments. Socioeconomic issues which plagued Black individuals in resource destitute environments would exacerbate as a result of legislation enacted under Reagan. Remaining consistent with the thesis of this analysis, the augmentation of Black inferiority as the premise of Reagan's domestic policy promulgation as well as tools to subvert the ascendance of class mobility among Black people in America must be observed. Amendments made to the Anti-Drug Abuse Act of 1986 further distorted the socioeconomic condition of Black people; this was also the same year amendments were made to the Military Cooperation with Civilian Law Enforcement Agencies Act of 1981. In corroboration, these domestic policy decisions envisaged further marginalization of the Black community by enacting stricter drug related penalties with the militarization of the police to aid and abet in the pretentious War on Drugs.

CHAPTER 18-MILITARY SUPPORT FOR CIVILIAN LAW ENFORCEMENT AGENCIES Sec. 381. Procurement by State and local governments of law enforcement equipment suitable for counter-drug activities through the Department of Defense.

§ 381. Procurement by State and local governments of law enforcement equipment suitable for counterdrug activities through the Department of Defense

---

[129] "The Controlled Substances Act: Overview."
[130] *Drugs of Abuse: a DEA Resource Guide.*
[131] Mark J Perry. "The Shocking Story behind Richard Nixon's 'War on Drugs' That Targeted Blacks and Anti-war Activists."
[132] Tom LoBianco. "Report: Nixon's War on Drugs Targeted Black People."
[133] Andrew Glass. "Reagan Declares 'War on Drugs,' October 14, 1982."

(a) *Procedures. - (1) The Secretary of Defense shall establish procedures in accordance with this subsection under which States and units of local government may purchase law enforcement equipment suitable for counter-drug activities through the Department of Defense. The procedures shall require the following:*

(A) *Each State desiring to participate in a procurement of equipment suitable for counter-drug activities through the Department of Defense shall submit to the Department, in such form and manner and at such times as the Secretary prescribes, the following:*
(i) *A request for law enforcement equipment.*

(ii) *Advance payment for such equipment, in an amount determined by the Secretary based on estimated or actual costs of the equipment and administrative costs incurred by the Department.*
(B) *A State may include in a request submitted under subparagraph (A) only the type of equipment listed in the catalog produced under subsection (c).*

(C) *A request for law enforcement equipment shall consist of an enumeration of the law enforcement equipment that is desired by the State and units of local government within the State. The Governor of a State may establish such procedures as the Governor considers appropriate for administering and coordinating requests for law enforcement equipment from units of local government within the State.*

(D) *A State requesting law enforcement equipment shall be responsible for arranging and paying for shipment of the equipment to the State and localities within the State.*[134]

Subtitle B—Drug Possession Penalty Act of 1986

SEC. 105L SHORT TITLE.
This subtitle may be cited as the "Drug Possession Penalty Act of 1986".

SEC. 1052. PENALTY FOR SIMPLE POSSESSION.

Section 404 of the Controlled Substances Act (21 U.S.C. 844) is amended to read as follows:

PENALTY FOR SIMPLE POSSESSION "SEC. 404.

(a) *It shall be unlawful for any person knowingly or intentionally to possess a controlled substance unless such substance was obtained directly, or pursuant to a valid prescription or order, from a practitioner, while acting in the course of his professional practice, or except as otherwise authorized by this title or title III. Any person who violates this subsection may be sentenced to a term of imprisonment of not more than 1 year, and shall be fined a minimum of $1,000 but not more than $5,000, or both, except that if he commits such offense after a prior conviction under this title or title III, or a prior conviction for any drug or narcotic offense chargeable under the law of any State, has become final, he shall be sentenced to a term of imprisonment for not less than 15 days but not more than 2 years, and shall be fined a minimum of $2,500 but not more than $10,000, except, further,*

---

[134] U.S. Congress. *United States Code: Military Cooperation with Civilian Law Enforcement Officials, 10 U.S.C. §§ 374-378*

that if he commits such offense after two or more prior convictions under this title or title III, or two or more prior convictions for any drug or narcotic offense chargeable under the law of any State, or a combination of two or more such offenses have become final, he shall be sentenced to a term of imprisonment for not less than 90 days but not more than 3 years, and shall be fined a minimum of $5,000 but not more than $25,000. The imposition or execution of a minimum sentence required.[135]

The focus on the demand side of the War on Drugs would also be reified by Democratic Party politicians as well. Although President Bill Clinton did not coin the phrase "tough on crime", it was this rhetoric which led to him signing the Violent Crime Control and Law Enforcement Act of 1994. Parallel to the judiciary mechanisms which incentivized the slave patrol to return runaway slaves to their owners, the federal government incentivized states to enact punitive and reactionary laws, while ensuring prisons remained full. In corroboration with a militarized police force established by Reagan, the Crime Bill would further cement the class inferiority of Black people in the United States. From 1995 to 2000 the federal government subsidized punitive legislation by allocating an aggregate amount of $7.9 billion to incentive grants.

TITLE II--PRISONS
Subtitle A--Violent Offender Incarceration and Truth in Sentencing Incentive Grants

SEC. 20102. TRUTH IN SENTENCING INCENTIVE GRANTS.

(a) Truth in Sentencing Grant Program.-- Fifty percent of the total amount of funds appropriated to carry out this subtitle for each of fiscal years 1995, 1996, 1997, 1998, 1999, and 2000 shall be made available for Truth in Sentencing Incentive Grants. To be eligible to receive such a grant, a State must meet the requirements of section 20101(b) and shall demonstrate that the State--

(1) has in effect laws which require that persons convicted of violent crimes serve not less than 85 percent of the sentence imposed; or
(2) since 1993—

(A) has increased the percentage of convicted violent offenders sentenced to prison;
(B) has increased the average prison time which will be served in prison by convicted violent offenders sentenced to prison;
(C) has increased the percentage of sentence which will be served in prison by violent offenders sentenced to prison; and
(D) has in effect at the time of application laws requiring that a person who is convicted of a violent crime shall serve not less than 85 percent of the sentence imposed if—

(i) the person has been convicted on 1 or more prior occasions in a court of the United States or of a State of a violent crime or a serious drug offense; and
(ii) each violent crime or serious drug offense was committed after the defendant's conviction of the preceding violent crime or serious drug offense.

(b) Allocation of Truth in Sentencing Incentive Funds.--
(1) Formula allocation.--The amount available to carry out this section for any fiscal year under subsection (a) shall be allocated to each eligible State in the ratio that the number of part 1 violent crimes reported by such State to the Federal Bureau of Investigation for 1993 bears to the number of part 1 violent crimes reported by all States to the Federal Bureau of Investigation for 1993.

---

[135] H.R.5484, 99th Congress (1985-1986)

(2) Transfer of unused funds.-- On September 30 of each of fiscal years 1996, 1998, 1999, and 2000, the Attorney General shall transfer to the funds to be allocated under section 20103(b)(1) any funds made available to carry out this section that are not allocated to an eligible State under paragraph (1).

SEC. 20109. AUTHORIZATION OF APPROPRIATIONS.
    There are authorized to be appropriated to carry out this subtitle--
    (1) $175,000,000 for fiscal year 1995;
    (2) $750,000,000 for fiscal year 1996;
    (3) $1,000,000,000 for fiscal year 1997;
    (4) $1,900,000,000 for fiscal year 1998;
    (5) $2,000,000,000 for fiscal year 1999; and
    (6) $2,070,000,000 for fiscal year 2000.[136]

The amalgamation of legislation and rhetoric from administrations focusing on the War on Drugs and the War on Crime proved to be disastrous for Black people. What Michelle Alexander has substantiated as the Prison Pipeline System demonstrates how the determination of the number of prisons needed stems from proficiency exams in elementary school. According to a study conducted by the Justice Policy Institute, in 1980 there were 143,000 Black men in jail or prison compared to 463,700 Black men enrolled in colleges or universities.[137] By the turn of the century, the study found that in 2000 there were 791,600 black men in jail or prison and 603,032 enrolled in colleges or universities.[138] Additionally, the study contends that the increase in the Black male prison population coincides with the prison construction boom that began 1980.[139] The relationship between the prison industrial complex and the Black community has been enabled by increased surveillance and patrol of Black communities by law enforcement as well as the judicial system.

The consortium between law enforcement, judicial appointees, and elected officials are incentivized by increased revenue generation to the city; the Black community is often the recipient of harassment based on the premise established of social hierarchy stemming from colonial and imperial ideologies. In 2015 an investigation of the Ferguson Police Department conducted by The United States Department of Justice – Civil Rights Division highlighted the extent to which similar propensities that incentivized the slave patrol to generate personal revenue has transcended into a strategy for local municipalities to expand their general fund budget. Throughout the duration of the investigation, the DOJ spent approximately 100 person-days onsite in Ferguson.[140] The department also participated in ride-alongs with on-duty officers, reviewed over 35,000 pages of police records as well as thousands of emails and other electronic materials provided by the police department.[141]

A summation of the investigation revealed that Ferguson's law enforcement practices are shaped by the City's focus on revenue rather than by public safety needs.[142]

---

[136] H.R. 3355, 103rd Congress (1993-1994)
[137] Fox Butterfield. "Study Finds Big Increase in Black Men as Inmates Since 1980."
[138] Ibid…,
[139] Ibid…,
[140] United States Department of Justice Civil Rights Division. "Investigation of the Ferguson Police Department - Justice." p.1
[141] Ibid…,
[142] United States Department of Justice Civil Rights Division. "Investigation of the Ferguson Police Department - Justice." p.2

Furthermore, Ferguson's own data establishes clear racial disparities that adversely impact Black people within the city limits.[143] The report highlighted how city officials routinely urged Former Chief of Police Tom Jackson to generate more revenue through enforcement. In March 2010, the City Finance Director, wrote to Chief Jackson contending: "unless ticket writing ramps up significantly before the end of the year, it will be hard to significantly raise collections next year... given that we are looking at a substantial tax shortfall, it is not an insignificant issue." Moreover, the in March 2013, the Finance Director wrote to the City Manager: "Court fees are anticipated to rise about 7.5%. I did ask the Chief if he thought the PD could deliver a 10% increase. He indicated that he could try." The report also demonstrated how pressure is placed on officers throughout the police department, and that message comes from City leadership.[144]

More purportedly, an analysis of police practices display how patrol assignments and schedules are geared toward aggressive enforcement of Ferguson's municipal code, with insufficient thought given to whether enforcement strategies promote public safety or unnecessarily undermine community trust and cooperation. Officer evaluations and promotions depend on an inordinate degree on "productivity," meaning the number of citations issued. Consequentially, as a result of the priorities of City officials and the Ferguson Police Department, many officers appeared to see some residents, especially those in Ferguson's Black communities, less as constituents to be protected than as potential offenders and sources of revenue.[145]

Racial disparities are also prevalent in Ferguson Police Department's use of force, of which 90% of documented use of force incidents was used against Black citizens. According to the report, in every canine bite incident for which racial information is available, the person bitten was Black. Additionally, the DOJ found substantial evidence of racial bias among police and court staff in Ferguson. During the investigation, emails surfaced which had been circulated by police supervisors and court staff which stereotype racial minorities as criminals, including one email joking about an abortion by a Black woman as being a means of crime control.[146]

Transcending into the tumultuous climate between the Black community and law enforcement contemporarily; episodes of civil disobedience have come as a response to the seemingly perpetual subordination emanating from public officials and law enforcement, which is also justified by legal statutes and legal processes. The consequences of Ronald Reagan's War on Drugs have created this pervasive dichotomy between law enforcement and the Black community which so no signs of ending. Instances such as the killing of Stephon Clark in 2018 by Sacramento Police Department have been endemic within the Black community throughout the United States as a result of over-policing. Police officers often patrol impoverished Black communities with a heightened sense of security because of the rhetoric exhorted during the War on Drugs. This rhetoric delineates Black individuals as being impulsive, lazy, dependent, and beastlike. To go even further, the rhetoric is also echoed by public officials like the District Attorney. In the case of Stephon Clark, Sacramento's district attorney conducted an individual investigation as

[143] United States Department of Justice Civil Rights Division. "Investigation of the Ferguson Police Department - Justice." p.2
[144] Ibid...,
[145] Ibid...,
[146] Ibid..., p.5

to whether the officers involved in Clark's killing to determine whether there was any criminal action involved in the shooting. The District Attorney's report was aimed in strictly observing whether there was sufficient evidence to charge the officers with a crime; a summation of the DA's report details: "The District Attorney's Office has completed an independent assessment of the above-referenced officer-involved shooting. Issues of civil liability, tactics, and departmental policies and procedures were not considered. We only address whether there is sufficient evidence to support the filing of criminal action in connection with the shooting of Stephon Clark. For the reasons set forth, we conclude that the shooting was lawful."

The DA contended however, that to gain a better legal understanding of Clark's actions leading up the shooting, it was important to uncover the details of his life prior to the event. As a result, the toxicology report uncovered the number of drugs that were in his system at the time of the shooting. The DA had the contents of his cell phone downloaded. This would be used to connect Clark's prior dealings with the police as well the mother of his children to the ostensible actions resulting in his death. The report highlighted text messages and calls to multiple people, including the mother of his children, former partners, and contacts who could provide him with drugs. The report also highlighted his google search contents, which uncovered searches on how to commit suicide. By framing it in this manner, the District Attorney posthumously killed the character of Stephon Clark. Amalgamating this information to the video and narrative of the police officers, the DA insinuated that Stephon Clark, intentionally used the police to commit suicide. Thereby justifying his death beyond the legal perspective of seeking to investigate the alleged criminality of the police officers involved in the shooting; the narrative shifted to focus on why Stephon Clark acted in the manner he did.

The ideologies which were historically used to justify Black subordination have not disappeared. It is ubiquitous within the rhetoric of academia, economics, law, and the minds of individuals with power. Within this article, the examination of colonial and imperial ideologies has been highlighted which were congenial to justify European expansion abroad. Following this rhetoric was the legal and economic observation of the inferiority of Black people. This led to chattel slavery, and colonialism. Domestically, the inception and adaptation of legal statutes, and tools of enforcement which have extended beyond generations and metabolized contemporarily has been observed. Yet, even after this illumination, the power dynamics still remain the same. This egregious rhetoric of inferior delineations has become so permeated into the consciousness of the colonized and neocolonial world that it has become subconscious in the examination of society's contemporary polarization. It has also "trickled down" to the pretentious solutions for the subordination of Black people within the United States, as well as Black people throughout the globe. The only answer to the neocolonial problems of Black people can be to repudiate propensities of neoliberalism and essentially neocolonialism which continue to be the antithesis to true traditional Afrikan thought and livelihood. Therefore, the only true way to subvert our subservience is to reject the system and create a more equal system based on the premise of humanity – Ubuntu.

People get used to anything. The less you think about your oppression, the more your tolerance for it grows. After a while, people just think oppression is the normal state of things. But to become free, you have to be acutely aware of being a slave. – Assata Shakur

If one is truly revolutionary, one must take time out to study. Because revolutionary theories are based on historical analyses, one must study. – Kwame Ture

Racism… is a universal operating system of white supremacy and domination in which the majority of the worlds white people participate. – Dr. Frances Cress Welsing

The restitution of Africa's humanist and egalitarian principles of society require socialism. – Kwame Nkrumah

Bibliography

"Anslinger, Harry Jacob, and U.S. Drug Policy." Encyclopedia of Drugs, Alcohol, and
    Addictive Behavior. *Encyclopedia.com.* (June 17, 2019).
    https://www.encyclopedia.com/education/encyclopedias-almanacs-transcripts-
    and-maps/anslinger-harry-jacob-and-us-drug-policy.

"The Controlled Substances Act: Overview." Findlaw.
    https://criminal.findlaw.com/criminal-charges/controlled-substances-act-csa-
    overview.html.

Avalon Project - Fugitive Slave Act 1850. Accessed June 26, 2019.
    https://avalon.law.yale.edu/19th_century/fugitive.asp.

Baradaran, Mehrsa. *The Color of Money: Black Banks and the Racial Wealth Gap.* Cambridge,
    MA: Belknap Press of Harvard University Press, 2017.

Beckert, Sven. *Empire of Cotton: A New History of Global Capitalism.* London: Penguin Books,
    2015.

Butterfield, Fox. "Study Finds Big Increase in Black Men as Inmates Since 1980." The
    New York Times. August 28, 2002.
    https://www.nytimes.com/2002/08/28/us/study-finds-big-increase-in-black-
    men-as-inmates-since-1980.html.

Digital History. Accessed June 26, 2019.
    http://www.digitalhistory.uh.edu/disp_textbook.cfm?smtID=3&psid=4035.

Drugs of Abuse: a DEA Resource Guide. U.S. Dept. of Justice, Drug Enforcement
    Administration, 2015.

Ekeh, Peter P. "Colonialism and the Two Publics in Africa: A Theoretical
    Statement." *Africa,* 2018, 87-109. doi:10.4324/9780429502538-7.

Glass, Andrew. "Reagan Declares 'War on Drugs,' October 14, 1982." POLITICO.
    October 14, 2010. https://www.politico.com/story/2010/10/reagan-declares-war-
    on-drugs-october-14-1982-043552.

H.R. 3490, 82nd Congress (1951–1952)

H.R.5484, 99th Congress (1985-1986)

H.R. 3355, 103rd Congress (1993-1994)

LoBianco, Tom. "Report: Nixon's War on Drugs Targeted Black People." *CNN.* March
    24, 2016. Accessed June 26, 2019.

https://www.cnn.com/2016/03/23/politics/john-ehrlichman-richard-nixon-drug-war-blacks-hippie/index.html.

Perry, Mark J. "The Shocking Story behind Richard Nixon's 'War on Drugs' That Targeted Blacks and Anti-war Activists." *AEI.* 2018. Accessed June 26, 2019. http://www.aei.org/publication/the-shocking-and-sickening-story-behind-nixons-war-on-drugs-that-targeted-blacks-and-anti-war-activists/.

Smith, Laura. "How a Racist Hate-monger Masterminded America's War on Drugs." *Timeline.com.* February 28, 2018. Accessed June 26, 2019. https://timeline.com/harry-anslinger-racist-war-on-drugs-prison-industrial-complex-fb5cbc281189.

U.S. Congress. *United States Code: Military Cooperation with Civilian Law Enforcement Officials, 10 U.S.C. §§ 374-378 Suppl. 2.* 1982. Periodical. https://www.loc.gov/item/uscode1982-028010018/.

U.S. Const. art. IV, § 2. (This clause is superseded by the 13th Amendment).

United States. 1956. *Narcotic control act of 1956. Report ... to accompany H.R. 11619, a bill to amend the Internal revenue code of 1954 and the Narcotic drugs import and export act to provide for a more effective control of narcotic drugs and marihuana, and for other purposes.* Washington: U.S. Govt. Print. Off.

United States Department of Justice Civil Rights Division. "Investigation of the Ferguson Police Department - Justice." Justice.Gov. March 4, 2015. https://www.justice.gov/sites/default/files/opa/press-releases/attachments/2015/03/04/ferguson_police_department_report.pdf.

Wolff, Edward. "How the Pie Is Sliced: America's Growing Concentration of Wealth." The American Prospect. August 1995. https://prospect.org/article/how-pie-sliced-americas-growing-concentration-wealth#fig07.

The Connection of Oppression: Cultural, Political, and Economic Domination by Western Nations Connecting the Necessity of Pan African Unity

Symbols of colonialism have extended beyond the 20th century and are now apparent in the 21st century. Emanating from western intellectual thought, colonialism has been metabolized and institutionalized through various forms which constitute neocolonialism. Profound African revolutionaries have delineated manners by which neocolonialism has been fostered on the African continent. What has yet to be outlined denotes the parallel propensities of neocolonialism within the United States upon the gaining of ostensible independence via the Emancipation Proclamation in 1863. Additionally, the examination of even more contemporary neocolonialism is being observed through urban developmental policies within metropolitan locations guided by the auspices of laissez-faire market fundamentalism and macroeconomic regulatory premises, otherwise known as economic neoliberalism. Free market orientation guiding the urban development political-economy has aided in the proliferation of gentrification as a characteristic of neocolonialism in an increasing globalized world. Kwame Nkrumah, Amilcar Cabral, Peter Ekeh, Frantz Fanon, and Fred Hampton, during their tenure, demonstrated how colonialism and successively neocolonialism has become aggrandized through various means. The factors congenial to neocolonial domination and neoliberal market fundamentalism appear contemporarily in evidence of apparently organic, recurring connections with powerful interests — such as financial and corporate factions, governmental and financial elites, dominant transnational agencies and institutions. Through economic, political, and cultural foreign domination, this essay will analyze how colonialism has transcended into neocolonialism in the United States, and throughout the continent of Africa, while analyzing the parallel political-economic environment spurring global gentrification.

Colonialism and Neocolonialism in Africa

The Berlin Conference of 1884-85 was the catalyst for the European partitioning of Africa. The demand for European expansion of industrial capitalism beyond their borders, as well as the need to safeguard their commercial interests were congenial to the agreement of arbitrary borders outlined by the colonial powers. Supporting Vladimir Lenin's theory of capitalist development leading to imperialism, the scramble for Africa was the epitome of imperialist domination transcending domestic borders. Hannah Arendt supports this stance contending:

> *Imperialism was born when the ruling class in a capitalist production came up against national limitations to it economic expansion. The bourgeois turned to politics out of economic necessity; for if it did not want to give up the capitalist system whose inherent law is constant growth, it had to impose this law upon its home governments and to proclaim expansion to be an ultimate goal of foreign policy.*[147]

Therefore, the legitimation of imperialist expansion as a foreign policy can be seen as an attempt for European powers to aggrandize the domestic economy by justifying their political-economic domination over the continent of Africa. Peter Ekeh delineates two distinct strategies Europeans nations used to justify their domination abroad: Imperial and

---

[147] Arendt, Hannah. *The Origins of Totalitarianism.*

Colonial ideologies of legitimation. Imperial ideologies emerged from the rhetoric exerted by colonizing nations to their citizens and taxpayers rationalizing and justifying the expansion.[148] Imperial ideologies were invented by the Europeans to persuade Africans that colonization was beneficial for them.[149] It is the establishment and permeation of these pre-colonial structures and auspices which would allow for the transition from colonialism to neocolonialism during the post-colonial period. Under the guise of subordination and underdevelopment, imperial ideologies contended that colonial rule was benign because, the history of African past was backward, and Africans needed saving from themselves; particularly their ancestor-worship.[150] As a result, missionaries were instrumental to extending colonial rule, by indoctrinating Africans with the perspectives of their colonizers. Missionaries openly told Africans that ancestor-worship was bad and that they should cut themselves loose from their 'evil' past and embrace the present in the new symbolisms of Christianity and Western Culture. In summation, Africans were told that the colonizers and missionaries came to save them…[151] This imperial ideology is important to understand because it is integral to the imposition of neocolonialism on the continent by metropole nations as well as the imposition of neocolonialism of emancipated persons in the United States. The United Kingdom and France were particularly successful in their colonial domination by corroborating colonial administrations and Christian Missionaries.

The hypocrisy of European colonial rhetoric as being advantageous to Africans lies therein the African economy. During colonialism, benefits from macroeconomic development solely went to metropole nations as commodities influenced by European demands were exported to Europe, and the exports profits invested in the domestic economy; microeconomic gains were stagnant if not depressional. The African economy, under colonial rule would be shaped by European interests through the implementation of a punitive tax system which would innately coerce African nations under colonial rule to become dependent. Another mechanism was the mechanism of monetization. The colonial powers introduced government-issued colonial currencies, often tied in value and exchangeability to colonial monetary units.[152] The monetization process served as a gateway for the colonizing nations to augment the tax system, which if attempted to evade paying had punitive punishment attached to it.[153]

In addition, western education was instrumental to cultural domination, and was usually a consortium with religious imposition. During the colonial epoch, to serve the metropole political-economy, the facets of European life became prolific through education. [154] It was through western educational institutions which aided in the proliferation of European written word, scientific principles, materialistic fetishism, and philosophic view of man's relation to society.[155]

Yet another instrumental point to aid in comprehending how colonial powers retained power during the post-colonial period. Substantiating the consortium between

---

[148] Peter P Ekeh. "Colonialism and the Two Publics in Africa: A Theoretical Statement." p.95
[149] Ibid…,
[150] Peter P Ekeh. "Colonialism and the Two Publics in Africa: A Theoretical Statement." p.97
[151] Ibid…,
[152] Moses Ochonu. "African Colonial Economies: State Control, Peasant Maneuvers, and Unintended Outcomes." p.8
[153] Moses Ochonu. "African Colonial Economies: State Control, Peasant Maneuvers, and Unintended Outcomes." p.8
[154] Walter Rodney. *How Europe Underdeveloped Africa* p.140
[155] Ibid…,

education and religious indoctrination is within the purview of Reverend Thomas Thompson, the first European educator on the Gold Coast (now Ghana), who wrote a pamphlet in 1778 titled, *The African Trade for Negro Slaves Shown to be Consistent with the Principles of Humanity and the Laws of Revealed Religion.*[156] It is through these individual mechanisms, often being interdependent which would allow for the percolation of neocolonialism throughout the continent; instrumental in understanding how colonial powers retained power during the post-colonial period.

The premise establishing the framework constituting neocolonialism and connecting it to propensities in the United States is the definition purported by Kwame Nkrumah:

> *The essence of neocolonialism is that the state which is subject to it is, in theory, independent and has all the trappings of international sovereignty. In reality it's economic system and thus its political system is directed from the outside.*[157]*… Though the aim of the neo-colonialists is economic domination, they do not confine their operations to the economic sphere. They use the old colonialist methods of religious, educational and cultural infiltration.*[158]

The Point Four program acted as the Marshall Plan for Africa. Contextually, the Marshall Plan was used to introduce the withering German economy to United States finance and industrial capital. Therefore, the Point Four program allowed the following financial institutions to dominate the monetary and fiscal sectors of the African economy:

> *Rockefeller, Morgan, Kuhn Loeb and Dillion Read institutions; the big British banks, Barclays, Lloyds, Westminster, Provincial, the investment houses pivoted around Hambros, Rothschild, Philip Hill; The Franch banks, Banque de Paris et das Pays Bas, Banque de l'Union Parisienne, Banque de l'Indochine, Union Européen Industrielle, Banque Worms, Crédit Lyonnais, Lazard Freres. Etc…*[159]

Colonialism as a foreign policy during the independence period was reshaped in a seemingly less egregious manner. Economically, the imperialists metaphysically transmuted their military, diplomatic, and administrative leverage into an infrastructural mechanism.[160] Nkrumah supports: "The aim of the imperialist power, in the application of their aid program[me]s, is to turn the State sector into an appendage of private capital… The declared basic policy of the Agency for International Development (formerly International Co-operation Administration) is to "employ United States assistance to aid-receiving countries in such a way as will encourage the development of the private sector of their economies."[161] The evidence for this strategy is substantiated when observing the exacerbation of socioeconomic issues within African nations upon receiving structural adjustment loans (SAL) issued by the US-controlled international finance institutions – the International Monetary Fund (IMF) and the World Bank. The stipulations for receiving a structural adjustment loan was the complete macroeconomic shift towards a free market oriented-neoliberal system. This system focused on reduced government spending, the opening of borders for trade and finance, and the aggrandization of the private sector. All

---

[156] Walter Rodney. *How Europe Underdeveloped Africa* p.141
[157] Kwame Nkrumah. *Neocolonialism: the Last Stage of Imperialism.* p.ix
[158] Ibid…, p.35
[159] Ibid…, p.61
[160] Ibid…, p.54
[161] Ibid…, p.55

of which would be advantageous for the imperial owners of finance and industrial capital to continue their control over the African economy.

In addition, foreign cultural domination enabled the colonizing nation to perpetuate its rule. As the indigenous population became endowed and proficient in European social structures and perspectives, the population is essentially assimilated to the influences, and therefore, the thought processes of the imperialists. Amilcar Cabral connects the domination of a people's culture to their economic environment:

> In fact, culture is always in the life of a society (open or closed), the more or less the conscious result of the economic and political activities of that society...[162] The experience of colonial domination shows that, in effort to perpetuate exploitation, the colonizers not only creates a system to repress cultural life of the colonized people; he also provokes and develops the cultural alienation of a part of the population, either by so called assimilation of indigenous people, or by creating a social gap between the indigenous elites and the popular masses.[163] History proves that it is much less difficult to dominate and continue dominating a people whose culture is similar or analogous to that of the conqueror.[164]...[I]t happens that a considerable part of the population, notably the urban or peasant petite bourgeoisie, assimilates to the colonizers mentality, considers itself culturally superior to its own people and ignores or looks down upon their cultural values.[165]

Foreign cultural domination was the goal of education African in European ideals. Under the guise of spreading civilization, the colonizers sought to assimilate indigenous Africans. According to the French, an African, after receiving French education, stood a chance of becoming an *assimilée* – one who could be assimilated or incorporated into the French superior culture.[166] This was imposed on Africans through establishment of European educational institutions in the late 19th century, of which were largely under the jurisdiction of Christian missionaries, and successively the church.[167] Moreover, French leaders understood the importance of cultural dominance in order to make their conquest easier.[168] They knew that if Africans became proficient in French language and culture then they would begin to identify as French. The first French educational institution named, *Alliance Française* – recognized by the French government would be instrumental in French entrenchment.[169] The intentions of this colonial extension were expressed by the founder of *Alliance Française,* Pierre Foncin, who has been quoted saying, "it is necessary to attach the colonies to the metropole by a very psychological bond, against the day when their progressive emancipation ends in language thought and spirit."[170]

The features of precolonial education in Africa emphasize social links between the environment, spirituality, and the communal relations to man within the community. Walter Rodney maintains, the features of indigenous African education retains a close link with social life, both in material and spiritual sense; its collective nature; its many sidedness; and its progressive development in conformity with the successive stages of physical, emotional, and mental development of the child.[171] Thus, the introduction of

---

[162] Amilcar Cabral. *Return to the Source; Selected Speeches.* p.41
[163] Amilcar Cabral. *Return to the Source; Selected Speeches.* p.45
[164] Ibid…, p.48
[165] Ibid…, p.45
[166] Walter Rodney. *How Europe Underdeveloped Africa.* p.247
[167] Ibid…, p.252
[168] Ibid…, p.256
[169] Ibid…,
[170] Ibid…, p.259
[171] Ibid…, p.239

European education did not introduce education to Africa, it reformed the principles of education to reflect colonizer perspectives and needs. Rodney contends, the main purpose of the colonial school systems was to perpetuate the social relationship of colonial society, tending to the needs of the colonial administration; Africans were trained to help facilitate operations at the lowest levels of local administrations and private capitalist firms.[172] Essentially, the colonizers imposed a capitalist educational relationship upon their colonies, bringing with them the caste system and a class bias encompassed with this socioeconomic relationship. It would be through this education system which would allow for the rise of indigenous petite bourgeoise.

According to Rodney, the church's role was primarily to preserve the social relations of colonialism, as an extension of the role it played in preserving the social relations of capitalism in Europe.[173] With the acceptance of capitalism as the structure for society, the theory of class ascendancy rises as well. Within colonial Africa, education – although misguided, marked the personal advancement within the structure created by European capitalists.[174] Wherein the capitalist education became the dominant socioeconomic relationship between African, it must be observed the degradation of community-oriented relationships – *Sankofa and Ubuntu*. Colonial education of capitalism instilled the premises of individualism and social alienation within the indigenous African population.[175] Individualism and cultural alienation is the complete antithesis to the African way of living; it would leave room for the manipulation of ethnic differences rather than reinforcing social solidarity. This can be observed within South Africa with the propagation of the Bantu Education act of 1953, which sought to promote differences between Zulu, Sotho, Xhosa, Venda, etc. tribes.

Amilcar Cabral, an astute revolutionary in Guinea-Bissau noted how the petite bourgeoisie come to consider themselves culturally superior upon assimilating to western culture. In a self-aggrandizing fashion, the petite bourgeoisie, after being educated by western schools on western doctrines perpetuate colonialism by regurgitating western ideals, often while repudiating European domination. Peter Ekeh contends: "anti-colonialism was against alien colonial personnel but was glaringly *pro* foreign ideals and principles."[176] The basis for petite bourgeoise rule was that they were just as proficient in western ideology, language, and bureaucracy, therefore they did not need to be under physical colonial rule.[177] This reasoning itself is the perpetuation of neocolonialism, as the petite bourgeoisie who was born out of colonial rule, is not sacrificial, and more so uncomfortable in being different than the colonizers, as they have granted ostensible freedom.[178] Essentially, the basis for legitimization of the petite bourgeoisie came from the legitimacy of European colonizers.

Thomas Sankara reifies the intentions of the colonial powers were not in the benevolent or humanitarian nature, but were used to produce a labor pool to their system

---

[172] Walter Rodney. *How Europe Underdeveloped Africa.* p.240
[173] Ibid…, p.253
[174] Ibid…, p.247
[175] Walter Rodney. *How Europe Underdeveloped Africa.* p.255
[176] Peter P Ekeh. "Colonialism and the Two Publics in Africa: A Theoretical Statement." p.101
[177] Ibid…, p.102
[178] Ibid…,

of exploitation.[179] Furthering this statement, Sankara contends that it is cheaper, easier, and more effective to achieve dominance through cultural commandeering.[180] Holistically, the imposition of European culture which assisted in the neo-colonizing of the African continent, through linguistic and religious conversion, as well as academic-intellectual indoctrination the structure of ideological domination would prove to be pervasive and enduring through decolonization.

The colonial powers came to realize that their efforts of continued military occupation in order continue their dominance would compromise the economic bearings of its domestic economy. France in particular realized the increased burden of the Franco-Algerian war. Through this, the Algerian government demanded full independence, not just decolonization. In return, the communist left of France would agree only to decolonization under the guise of maintaining special links the former colony. This was manipulative as Frantz Fanon highlights how their true interests were revealed upon negotiations. As the colonialist were forced to retreat from Algeria, their economic interests were most important issues within negotiation: banks, monetary areas, research permits, commercial concessions, inviolability of properties stolen from the peasants at the time of conquest etc.[181] Within the confines of arbitrarily outlined borders, Fanon describes this acceptance of neocolonialism as *nominal sovereignty.*[182]

> *The acceptance of a nominal sovereignty and the absolute refusal of real independence–such is the typical reaction of the colonialist nations with respect to their former colonies. Neocolonialism is impregnated with a few ideas which both constitute its force and at the same time prepare its necessary decline...[183] [Neo-colonialism] takes advantage of this inter-determination. Armed with a revolutionary and spectacular good will, it grants the former colony everything. But in so doing, it wrings from it an economic dependence which becomes an aid and assistance program.[184]*

In tandem with the establishment of a dependent economic relationship to France, newly independent nations including Algeria adopted the French constitution. The implications of this amalgamate the political, economic, and cultural dominance by colonial powers. The adoption of this legislative contract established a Franco-African Community which alienates the African personality and, establishes a single nationality.[185] The contentions of this relationship lies within the dialectical differences between cultures, socioeconomic statuses, and struggles between the colonizers and the Africans. Fanon explains the predicament:

> *Participating in the vote mean tacitly recognizing oneself as a member of the same family, of the same nation having common problems, whereas in reality each African who votes in the referendum will bind his people and his country a little more closely to French colonialism.[186]*

This special linkage envisaged by France inextricably linked the ostensibly independent nation to its former metropole. Additionally, as highlighted by Fanon, this relationship undermines the efforts of real independence while attempting to assimilate

---

[179] Thomas Sankara. *Thomas Sankara Speaks the Burkina Faso Revolution, 1983-1987.* p.223
[180] Thomas Sankara. *Thomas Sankara Speaks the Burkina Faso Revolution. 1983-1987.* p.197
[181] Frantz Fanon, and Haakon Chevalier. *Towards the African Revolution: Political Essays.* p.121
[182] Ibid...,
[183] Frantz Fanon, and Haakon Chevalier. *Towards the African Revolution: Political Essays.* p.121
[184] Ibid...,
[185] Ibid..., p.133
[186] Ibid...,

Africans to French culture by recognizing one nationality. The basis of analysis by the French displays the lack of observance for self-determination because it subverts the expansionist foreign policy of colonialism which benefits only the metropole economy. Moreover, the relationship illustrates how white supremacy within the liberal stance blossoms when faced with matters coinciding with self-interests. Recognizing the brutality of colonialism, yet not allowing for complete cultural, economic, and political independence is the epitome of perpetuating colonialism.

Colonialism and Neocolonialism in the United States

As the connection of colonialism and neocolonialism extends beyond the continent of Africa to the America's, the domination of enslaved Africans culturally, economically, and politically shares the same strategy and legitimation if imposition and indoctrination. Understanding that colonialism wasn't imposed in the same manner over enslaved Africans in the United States as it was over the domination of African indigenous land, it must be defined to the precariousness of European importation of property to occupied indigenous land in the Americas. The delineation of enslaved Africans as property establishes the dichotomizing relationship between the master and the enslaved, thus forming an enemy and ally relationship. Abstractly, "colonialism is an instance of a more general phenomenon of domination. Events that happened in the past, such as those in the period of colonial conquest and control, can provide insights into processes of domination and resistance in the present."[187]

The lamination of African subordination was established upon their utilization as financial instruments. However, a system of control had to be established. Slave holders sought to make enslaved Africans docile, and easier to conquer by stripping away the cultural beliefs brought over from the continent. In considering enslaved Africans as property, slave owners and traders stripped Africans of their cultural heritage. Africans who survived the brutal middle passage were further dehumanized upon landing in the New World. In African culture, there is an emphasis on the relationship between the community and the environment, aspects of nature were often given a name which had spiritual significance. According to the teachings of African spirituality, "when one bestows a name upon a child that person is not simply naming the flesh of the child, but rather the name is for the person's soul."[188] In that manner, names have been an important aspect of African culture and to remove that from the spirit of enslaved Africans was a process of cultural domination. In Catherine Adams and Elizabeth Pleck's *Love of Freedom,* a mention was made about how slave-owners in New England went about naming their enslaved populations:

> *At least among the slaves initially brought to New England, it was common for masters to assign their property new names – in this case, Hagar Blackmore, which meant slave woman of African descent. A name was the link to one's past, to a lineage; providing this woman with a new name was part of the dehumanization of slavery, erasing her previous identity and substituting one chosen by an owner.[189]*

---

[187] Viviane Salwh-Hanna, and Chris Affor. *Colonial Systems of Control: Criminal Justice in Nigeria.* p.33

[188] Samaki. *African Names: Reclaim Your Heritage.* p.7

[189] Catherine Adams, and Elizabeth H. Pleck. *Love of Freedom: Black Women in Colonial and Revolutionary New England.* p.7

This is not saying that all aspects of African culture were repressed. In fact, many aspects of African culture were retained, and adapted to the European culture which was being imposed on them. The most prominent feature was the utilization of music as a form of communication and resistance. Drums have historically been instrumental within African culture, and it is of no surprise that they were used as a secrete language to coordinate and facilitate rebellions.[190] The most notorious rebellion which led to the ubiquitous banning of drums was the Stono Revolt in South Carolina in 1739. An official account of the uprising states that there were several enslaved Africans "calling out Liberty… [They] marched on with Colours displayed and two Drums beating, pursuing all the white people they met.…They [the number of slaves] increased every minute…Singing and beating Drums to draw more Negroes to them."[191] The Negro Law of South Carolina was a legislative response to the Stono Revolt. In summation, the legislation asserts that if any plantation owner was caught allowing enslaved Africans to congregate, beat drums, or use any loud instruments, then the plantation, slaves, and assets of the plantation owner would be seized.[192]

On the plantation, attempts were made to pacify enslaved African through religious instruction. The importance of creating docile enslaved populations was to maximize the efficiency of southern region's economy. The was result of this demand caused an instructional document to proliferate throughout the planter class. Dr. Reverend Charles Colock Jones supplied the need to pacify enslaved population through his work *How to Make a Negro Christian The Religious Instruction of the Negroes and Other Works*. Much like the missionaries on the continent, the religious instruction of Dr. Reverend Jones intended to ostensibly save Africans from themselves, and relinquish them of sin. It reinforced the stance that it was of divine prophecy of enslaved peoples that they must be obedient to their master as it is the Christian Duty.[193] The religious text instructed the teachers to, "induce a sense of guilt, [they] must charge upon the negros those particular sins to which they are so much addicted…Many of them are guilty of notorious sins and know not that they are sins at all."[194]

The religious imposition of Christianity onto Africans didn't end with the signing of the emancipation proclamation. Instead, the religious indoctrination via the education system acted as a gateway for the economic indoctrination of capitalism to fulfil the labor needs of the southern economy during reconstruction. What is overlooked in the history of Black people in the United States after the civil war is the educational influence of missionaries and pretentious philanthropic northern industrialists post emancipation.

As the Union army defeated Confederate troops, they proliferated the enaction of the Emancipation Proclamation ostensibly granting the freedom to the enslaved. As northern troops traveled throughout the south, the missionaries followed them as well.[195] The missionaries were instrumental to educating, and indoctrinating freedman in northern

---

[190] "The Yale Historical Review." p.24

[191] Ibid…,

[192] Full text of "The Negro Law of South Carolina".

[193] Charles Colcock Jones, and Kamau Makesi-Tehuti. *How to Make a Negro Christian: a Reprinting of The Religious Instruction of the Negroes and Other Works*. p.53

[194] Charles Colcock Jones, and Kamau Makesi-Tehuti. *How to Make a Negro Christian: a Reprinting of The Religious Instruction of the Negroes and Other Works*. p.55

[195] E. Franklin Frazier. *Black Bourgeoisie*. p.60

ideals of industry and thrift.[196] Sociologist E. Franklin Frazier maintains "the first missionary expedition to propagate industry, religion, and education among the contrabands at Hilton Head (South Carolina), as well as encourage agriculture and like useful measures."[197] Northern philanthropic foundations began to fund Black education in the south within two of the abolition of slavery.[198] Philanthropic efforts by northern capitalists can be paralleled to the pretentious humanitarian efforts by missionaries on the continent who's intention was to influence Africans to identify as European.

In 1905, a wealthy Quaker woman in Philadelphia established the Jeanes Fund with a gift of $200,000 to aid in 'little county schools' for negros. Five years later the Phelps-Stokes Fund was established for the improvement of Negro education. Before this Fund was setup, the General Education Board, which was established in 1903 by John D. Rockefeller, began to aid Negro education in the South. By 1914 the General Education Board had contributed $700,000 to Negro schools."[199] It was through the General Education Board that Spelman College was made prestigious – named after Laura Spelman Rockefeller. Morehouse College, initially named Augusta Institute was created to educate Black men for careers in ministry and teaching. At the urging of the Rev. Frank Quarles, the school moved to Atlanta's Friendship Baptist Church in 1879 and changed its name to Atlanta Baptist Seminary.[200] During the tenure of the College's first African American president, John Hope, the College was renamed Morehouse College in 1913, in honor of Henry L. Morehouse, corresponding secretary of the National Baptist Home Missionary Society.[201] Upon further research, it was revealed that Andrew Carnegie contributed $600,000 to Tuskegee Institute, and provided lifetime income to the family of Booker T. Washington.[202]

Moreover, Frazier maintains that northern industrialists were not genuinely interested in educating Black people to augment their socioeconomic status. Much like the circumstances under colonial rule in Africa, freedmen were being educated to fulfill a laboring class and taught to identify as American. To this, Frazier asserts that home economics and domestic science were favored subjects because they were supposed to train Negros to become cooks for white people.[203] In assimilating Black people in the United States, the education schools emphasized the exhibition of proficiency in the English dialect; essentially repudiating the "broken" dialect of Black culture.[204]

Dr. Amos Wilson substantiates these claims as well. He provides more context to illuminate how influential missionary and industrial philanthropic colleges were to Black education in the south. He supports: "[A]s late as 1930 Black church organizations-controlled colleges which enrolled 14 percent of Black students. Missionary and industrial philanthropy-controlled colleges enrolled 61 percent of those students. The Black state and

---

[196] E. Franklin Frazier. *Black Bourgeoisie.* p.60
[197] Ibid…, p.61
[198] Ibid…, p.65
[199] Ibid…, p.66
[200] Morehouse College. "Morehouse." Morehouse College | Morehouse Legacy.
[201] Ibid…,
[202] "$600,000 FOR TUSKEGEE AND B.T. WASHINGTON; Andrew Carnegie's Contribution to the Endowment Fund. Also to Provide Life Income for Mr. and Mrs. Washington -- Philanthropist Has Been Giving $10,000 a Year to the Institute."
[203] E. Franklin Frazier. *Black Bourgeoisie.* p.70
[204] Ibid…, p.77

land grant colleges enrolled most of the remaining 25 percent."[205] Wilson expands on the utilization of education as means to stabilize the southern economy by creating an industrial and agricultural working class. 'Negro industrial training' was recognized by northern industrialists as the most appropriate education for Blacks in the south.[206]

On the aspect of cultural domination Wilson's rhetoric echoes the voice of Thomas Sankara and Frantz Fanon. With regards to stride for complete freedom of rule he denotes:

Even the nominal citizenship of Blacks in this white nation means a sacrifice of "Black power" since full membership in that nation would require Blacks to no longer see themselves as Black; that they shed their identity and consciousness of themselves as a people with cultural and other interests separate from those of whites.[207]

In essence, it is this same lack of control over the institutions which were built to assimilate Black people by the same class which benefitted from colonial enslavement that laid the ground for the perpetuation of colonialism. The next stage of colonialism would dictate the economic bearings of the Black community – in the same manner the perpetuation of colonialism burgeoned in Africa upon independence.

The drawing of arbitrary borders in Africa as a result of the Berlin Conference to legally protect the commercial interests of the colonizing nations can be observed more microeconomically within the United States during the suburbanization period. Upon initial glance the propensity of redlining mirrors the partitioning of land to segregate Black communities from white communities. Further analysis shows how this was reinforced by the presumption of racial hierarchy as well as the interests of commercial businesses. Widespread suburbanization occurred as a result of New Deal reform policies propagated by President Franklin Delano Roosevelt. His policies sough to address the housing shortage by creating governmental institutions which would insure and subsidize mortgages. However, financial institutions in consortium with the colonial United States government were culpable in these practices as well.

Redlining burgeoned the usage of an appraisal system by the Home Owners Loan Corporation (HOLC), a government sponsored corporation.[208] HOLC appraisers aggregated census data and survey results in order to predict how homes would appreciate.[209] The data collected would be used to create to delineate a categorized color-coded risk aversion map of neighborhoods.[210] The categories were, A(green), B(blue), C (yellow), and D(red).[211] Neighborhoods categorized as green were the most desirable and were homogeneously white, while red neighborhoods were largely Black.[212] The banking industry also utilized these maps to create residential security maps, referring to this "tool" when deciding where to lend.[213] Arbitrarily drawing borders through redlining relegated

[205] Amos N. *Blueprint for Black Power: a Moral, Political, and Economic Imperative for the Twenty-First Century*. p.189
[206] Ibid…, p.191
[207] Ibid…, p.205
[208] Mehrsa Baradaran. *The Color of Money: Black Banks and the Racial Wealth Gap*. p.105
[209] Ibid…,
[210] Ibid…,
[211] Mehrsa Baradaran. *The Color of Money: Black Banks and the Racial Wealth Gap*. p.105
[212] Ibid…,
[213] Ibid…, 106

Black people to be able to only live in certain areas within metropolitan areas. The connection between neocolonialism on the continent and in the United States is present as neither populaces had control over the boundaries nor the systems that controlled them within these boundaries.

Black owned homes were not afforded the ability to appreciate and create equity as were white owned homes. In fact, the characteristics of this neocolonialism ensured the value of the neighborhood deteriorated. The public sector ensured this by changing zoning delegations from residential to industrial upon the introduction of Black home ownership to the neighborhood.[214] This would also stunt Black home ownership, as banks and the Federal Housing Administration (FHA) rendered Black families ineligible for insured amortized mortgages because the area was designated as an industrial neighborhood.[215] The institutions considered the existence of nearby rooming houses, commercial development, or industry to create risk to the property value of single family homes, which were often white.[216] Moreover, Black neighborhoods were often the sites of toxic waste facilities and dumps – determined by the local municipality. It is of no coincidence that in Richmond, California, the area which had been historically Black because of the great migration – North Richmond – houses the Chevron Refinery (which has frequent fires that exacerbate health conditions of local residents) as well as the city dump, and many other industrial businesses.

Gentrification as Neocolonialism

The deterioration of Black neighborhoods trough the era of Redlining has allowed for the engendering of a more contemporary form of colonialism called gentrification. Gentrification is the neocolonial-settler colonial result occurring from macroeconomic urban renewal policies displacing low-income populations – known as economic neoliberalism; Black residents are often the most affected demographic. The erosion of communal relations and the displacement of low-income individuals are an afterthought in place for urban development policies that seek to attract direct investment in an attempt to revitalize the community. The conditions faced by local residents are the results of racist policies such as redlining, segregation, and over-policing. Legitimized by the state apparatus and capitalist finance institutions, these de jure and de facto practices created a dependency relationship between people in the periphery of the local economy and the state apparatus.

The premise of the economic neoliberal position is financial liberalization, privatization, slashing of government spending (austerity), and the cultivation of a business climate ripe for inward capital investments. David Harvey asserts the state's role is to create and preserve an institutional framework as characterized above.[217] The state has to guarantee the quality and integrity of money; it must also setup the military, defense, police, and legal structures required to secure private property rights and to guarantee, by force if need be, the proper functioning of markets.[218] In Africa, the imposition of

---

[214] Mehrsa Baradaran. *The Color of Money: Black Banks and the Racial Wealth Gap.* p.50
[215] Ibid…,
[216] Ibid…,
[217] Frank J. Lechner, and John Boli. *Globalization Reader.* p.71
[218] Frank J. Lechner, and John Boli. *Globalization Reader.* p.71

Structural Adjustment Programs (SAPs) allowed for the privatization and commandeering of the African Economy under the purview of a free market-oriented economy. Similarly, these policies are apparent when analyzing gentrification in Sacramento, California. The idea of New Market Tax Credits (NMTCs), and Opportunity Zones, are propensities contributing to growing gentrification. In fact, the propagation of Opportunity Zones can be traced to President Nixon who was a supporter of laissez-faire economics.[219] The rhetoric reinforces trickledown economics; contending that the means to lift populations out of poverty was to incentivize, and encourage private developers to invest in downtrodden communities (those affected by redlining, over-policing, and mass incarceration), resulting in the ostensible creation of jobs while the developer benefits from deferring taxes on capital gains throughout the longevity of investment holdings. However in 1995, a study conducted by the British government on the efficacy of enterprise zones concluded that tax-break incentivized policies do work to spur investment, but do not create jobs and do not lift people out of poverty.[220] Additionally, an article posted by *Forbes* reinforces the statement that financial gains of Opportunity Zones largely benefit the investor relative to the community.[221]

Already, the consequences of these neoliberal policies appear in the disproportionate amount of Black people within the homeless population. An article published by the *SacBee* shows how Black people, although making up 13 percent of the county's population, makeup 34 percent of the homeless population.[222] This is the result of rising rents associated with redevelopment, pressure from Bay Area migration, and the inflation of prices on consumer goods accompanied by stagnant wages. Since displacement is inherent to gentrification – by definition, the removal of a lower class for a more affluent group of people, the connection between colonial domination of a territory and gentrification of a community is inextricably linked to neoliberal-neocolonial policies.

Gentrification has been ubiquitous throughout the United States. Exuberant rents and housings costs have caused large demographic change in urban cities. In California, Oakland has realized the most precipitous decline in its Black population. A local newspaper, the *SFGate* reports that United States census shows a population decline of 25 percent of its Black population.[223] The exodus left the city with a net loss of 33,000 Black residents and made Oakland one of the few big California cities to decline in size.[224] Surrounding cities like Richmond and Berkeley have been affected by expanding gentrification. According the *Eastbayexpress,* in the year 2000, Black people numbered about 14,000, or 13 percent of the City of Berkeley's population.[225] Today, their numbers have fallen to approximately 9,700, and by 2030, the city's Black residents could number just 7,000 — just 5 percent of the total.[226] In Richmond, one third of Black residents have left over the past 15 years, dropping from 35,000 to 23,000. If this continues at the same

[219] Mehrsa Baradaran. "The Real Roots of 'Black Capitalism'."
[220] Communities and Local Government. "Final Evaluation of Enterprise Zones."
[221] Morgan Simon. "Opportunity Zones: We're Doing It Wrong."
[222] Alexandra Yoon-Hendricks, and Theresa Clift. "Up 19%, Homelessness in Sacramento County Hits 5,570. Officials 'Frustrated' but Hopeful."
[223] Matthai Kuruvilla. "25% Drop in African American Population in Oakland."
[224] Ibid…,
[225] Darwin Bondgraha. "The East Bay's Changing Demographics."
[226] Ibid…,

rate, Richmond's Black population might drop from 35 percent of the total population to just 11 percent by 2030.[227]

As the world becomes informally smaller through interdependence and increasing globalization, gentrification has spread beyond the borders of the United States. The amalgamation of neoliberal economic stances and intercontinental connections has led to the enhancement of global capital markets, and a transnational capitalist class (TCC). As defined by Leslie Sklair, the TCC is transnational in at least five senses:

> [I]ts members tend to share global as well as local economic interests; they seek to exert economic control in the workplace, political control in domestic and international politics, and culture-ideology control in everyday life; they tend to have global rather than local perspectives on a variety of issues; they tend to be people from many countries…; and they tend to share similar lifestyles, particularly patterns of luxury consumption of goods and services.[228]

As a result of neoliberal nuances, bureaucrats promulgate policy to create an environment allowing for the owners of capital (the TCC) to invest-in and develop their jurisdictions. The most notorious symbols of these policies arise through mechanisms to boost consumption, spreading the consumerist ideology needed to fuel the Transnational Capitalist Class. Suitably, the policies result in the construction of either: shopping malls, tourist attractions-destinations, and/or an arena for a major league sports team. Constructing these entities is an attempt for bureaucrats to augment their region into the global market financially and physically.

Since the role of the state is to preserve the institutions sanctioning the pompous free market for the transnational capitalist class, the state retracts itself as a provider of social support for lower-income populations, and in return reciprocates efforts towards supplying business services and amenities for a more affluent population.[229]

Cape Town, South Africa

Gentrification throughout South Africa has qualities distinct to the Western World as well as its own domestic economy. The macroeconomic framework taken up by local municipalities, and their state governments – within a capitalist society – assumes that poverty alleviation will come with economic growth. South Africa has followed this model as its strategy to address widespread poverty has been to aggressively grow the economy, with the goal to also augment its metropolitan areas into globally competitive cities; focusing on the cities of Cape Town, Durban, Johannesburg, and Pretoria.[230]

In July 1999, the Cape Town Partnership (CTP) was established. Comprised of representatives from the Cape Town's City Council, Cape Metro Council, the South African Property Owners Association, and various private businesses, the CTP was to lead and manage the regeneration of Cape Town's central city and promote it as a destination for global business, investment retail, and entertainment and leisure, thus promoting the

---

[227] Darwin Bondgraha. "The East Bay's Changing Demographics."
[228] Frank J. Lechner, and John Boli. *Globalization Reader.* p.68
[229] Ronnie Donaldson, Nico Kotze, Gustav Visser, Jinhee Park, Nermine Wally, Janaina Zen, and Olola Vieyra. "An Uneasy Match: Neoliberalism, Gentrification and Heritage Conservation in Bo-Kaap, Cape Town, South Africa." p.174
[230] Gustav Visser, and Nico Kotze. "The State and New-Build Gentrification in Central Cape Town, South Africa." p.2573

city into the global market.[231] The success of the CTP in the realm of economic development led to the specification of 'urban development zones'.[232] Similar to the macroeconomic policy guiding opportunity zones in the United States urban development zones incentivized private developers through tax credits and deferments in order to construct and improve building stock.[233] The unequal wealth and income distribution stemming from the oppressive reality under apartheid South Africa still has its vestiges. Much like Jim Crow policies and the effects of redlining on Black people in the United States, the policies of South Africa which were based on racial grounds have been institutionalized under neoliberal regimes. According to Gustav Visser and Nico Kotze, it appears as if these policies have been replaced by a financially exclusive property market that entrenches prosperity and privilege, and extends it to foreign investors, business entrepreneurs and vacationers.[234]

Lagos, Nigeria

Gentrification in Lagos, the former capitol of Nigeria shares the same characteristics of urban planning stemming from a colonial government that affected Black populations in the United States. The capitalist ideology of colonial urban space matches the rhetoric exerted by neoliberal stances, contending that in order for a market to run efficiently, public expenditure be kept to the barest minimum, that included municipal planning and administration.[235]

Under the rule of Britain, the colonial government in order to attract new residents to the heavily denigrated city, enacted the Lagos Town Planning Ordinance of 1927.[236] This ordinance as well as the policies enacted therein resulted in the same characteristics of segregation, housing degradation, and subversion of economic control striking Black people in the United States during the New Deal and suburbanization era. The Lagos Town Planning Ordinance established the Lagos Executive Development Board (LEDB) which was intended to make provision for the replanning, improvement and development of Lagos.[237] Similar to the strategies of the United States, replanning and development meant slum clearing, and the bulldozing of buildings. The Lagos central planning scheme of 1951 ensured the clearing and redevelopment of 20 acres of slum dwelling for the people who had been displaced from the various planning schemes of the 1930s, 1940s and 1950s, who were then to be relocated at Surulere.[238] (Surulere is a residential and commercial Local Government Area located on the mainland of Lagos). By 1955, 913 dwellings had been provided at Surulere and all had been occupied by 1962. The displaced population could not be accommodated at the original location; and the tenants, who occupied various rented apartments all over Lagos and who constituted a large percentage of the population, were inevitably evicted.[239]

---

[231] Gustav Visser, and Nico Kotze. "The State and New-Build Gentrification in Central Cape Town, South Africa." p.2575
[232] Ibid…, p.2577
[233] Ibid…,
[234] Gustav Visser, and Nico Kotze. "The State and New-Build Gentrification in Central Cape Town, South Africa." p.2585
[235] Lanre Davies. "Gentrification in Lagos, 1929–1990." p.726
[236] Ibid…, p.718
[237] Ibid…,
[238] Ibid…, 719
[239] Ibid…, 720

Conclusion

As I was writing this paper, I was also reading a book titled *Colonial Systems of Control* by Viviane Saleh-Hanna. She argues that Nkrumah's explanation of neocolonialism is correct, however the word itself (neocolonialism) is wrong as it assumes that colonialism on the continent has been repudiated and has come back in some *new* (neo) form. She maintains that colonialism on the continent is not new as it is the same structures extending the colonial regime into another century, and that the only new-colonial transitions have been European; this form of colonialism Saleh-Hanna has delineated as euphemized colonialism. Additionally, her excellency Ambassador Arikana Chihombori-Quao, the Permanent Representative of the African Union Representational Mission to the United States often tells of how the Berlin Conference is still alive today as we still recognize the arbitrary borders drawn by colonial powers and speak the languages of the colonizers. They both will contend that the face of colonialism has only changed today. Saleh-Hanna asserts that in today's world the oppressors come to us as friends and allies: Western funding agencies, international diplomatic allies, European colleagues who control organizational agendas, and fellow human rights activists who work to reinforce European economic and political structures and institutions, thereby working to make colonial institutions run more efficiently.

This paper has analyzed how Saleh-Hanna's explanation is exact and even extends that assertion to the condition Black people in the United States. Through foreign cultural, political, and economic domination the colonizing nations utilizing the same tools and mechanisms were able to dominate a numerically larger population of people. The premise of the Pan-African stance is that Black people globally share the same struggle and therefore share the same destiny. The struggle has been and will continue to be a fight against imperialist-neocolonial powers no matter who it may be so that we – as global Black people, and children of Africa – may realize our power in unity.

Bibliography

"$600,000 FOR TUSKEGEE AND B.T. WASHINGTON; Andrew Carnegie's Contribution to the Endowment Fund. Also to Provide Life Income for Mr. and Mrs. Washington -- Philanthropist Has Been Giving $10,000 a Year to the Institute." The New York Times. The New York Times, April 24, 1903. https://www.nytimes.com/1903/04/24/archives/600000-for-tuskegee-and-bt-washington-andrew-carnegies-contribution.html.

"The Yale Historical Review." Accessed October 30, 2019. http://historicalreview.yale.edu/sites/default/files/spring_2011_0.pdf.

Adams, Catherine, and Elizabeth H. Pleck. *Love of Freedom: Black Women in Colonial and Revolutionary New England.* Oxford: Oxford University Press, 2010.

Arendt, Hannah. *The Origins of Totalitarianism. Imperialism.* San Diego, NY, London: Harcourt Brace, 1985.

Baradaran, Mehrsa. "The Real Roots of 'Black Capitalism'." The New York Times. The New York Times, March 31, 2019. https://www.nytimes.com/2019/03/31/opinion/nixon-capitalism-blacks.html.

Baradaran, Mehrsa. *The Color of Money: Black Banks and the Racial Wealth Gap.* Cambridge, MA: The Belknap Press of Harvard University Press, 2017.

Bondgraha, Darwin. "The East Bay's Changing Demographics." East Bay Express. East Bay Express, October 30, 2019. https://www.eastbayexpress.com/oakland/the-east-bays-changing-demographics/Content?oid=13262928.

Cabral Amílcar. *Return to the Source; Selected Speeches.* New York: Monthly Review Press, 1974.

Communities and Local Government. "Final Evaluation of Enterprise Zones." Final evaluation of Enterprise Zones - Cities and regions. Communities and Local Government, November 4, 2008. https://webarchive.nationalarchives.gov.uk/ /http://www.communities.gov.uk/archived/general-content/citiesandregions/finalevaluation/.

Davies, Lanre. "Gentrification in Lagos, 1929–1990." *Urban History* 45, no. 4 (2018): 712–32. https://doi.org/10.1017/s0963926817000670.

Donaldson, Ronnie, Nico Kotze, Gustav Visser, Jinhee Park, Nermine Wally, Janaina Zen, and Olola Vieyra. "An Uneasy Match: Neoliberalism, Gentrification and Heritage Conservation in Bo-Kaap, Cape Town, South Africa." *Urban Forum* 24, no. 2 (2012): 173–88. https://doi.org/10.1007/s12132-012-9182-9.

Ekeh, Peter P. "Colonialism and the Two Publics in Africa: A Theoretical Statement." *Comparative Studies in Society and History* 17, no. 1 (January 1975): 91-112. doi:10.4324/9780429502538-7.

Fanon, Frantz, and Haakon Chevalier. *Towards the African Revolution: Political Essays.* New York: Grove Press, 1988.

Frazier, E. Franklin. *Black Bourgeoisie.* New York: Free Press Paperbacks, 1997.

Full text of "The Negro Law of South Carolina". Accessed October 31, 2019. https://archive.org/stream/negrolawsouthca00goog/negrolawsouthca00goog_djvu.txt.

Jones, Charles Colcock, and Kamau Makesi-Tehuti. *How to Make a Negro Christian: a Reprinting of The Religious Instruction of the Negroes and Other Works.* United States: Bolekaja Enterprises, 2006.

Kuruvila, Matthai. "25% Drop in African American Population in Oakland." SFGate. San Francisco Chronicle, January 11, 2012. https://www.sfgate.com/bayarea/article/25-drop-in-African-American-population-in-Oakland-2471925.php.

Lechner, Frank J., and John Boli. *Globalization Reader.* Wiley Blackwell, 2015.

Morehouse College. "Morehouse." Morehouse College | Morehouse Legacy. Accessed October 31, 2019. https://www.morehouse.edu/about/legacy.html.

Nkrumah, Kwame. *Neocolonialism: the Last Stage of Imperialism.* London: Panaf, 1971.

Rodney, Walter. *How Europe Underdeveloped Africa (23rd March 1942-13th June 1980).* London: Bogle-LOuverture Publications, 1988.

Saleh-Hanna, Viviane, and Chris Affor. *Colonial Systems of Control: Criminal Justice in Nigeria.* Ottawa: University of Ottawa Press, 2008.

Samaki. *African Names: Reclaim Your Heritage.* Cape Town: Struik Publishers, 2001.

Sankara, Thomas. *Thomas Sankara Speaks the Burkina Faso Revolution, 1983-1987.* New York, NY: Pathfinder, 2017.

Simon, Morgan. "Opportunity Zones: We're Doing It Wrong." Forbes. Forbes Magazine, September 3, 2019. https://www.forbes.com/sites/morgansimon/2019/09/03/opportunity-zones-were-doing-it-wrong/#73081a3656fa.

Visser, Gustav, and Nico Kotze. "The State and New-Build Gentrification in Central Cape Town, South Africa." *Urban Studies* 45, no. 12 (2008): 2565–93. https://doi.org/10.1177/0042098008097104.

Wilson, Amos N. *Blueprint for Black Power: a Moral, Political, and Economic Imperative for the Twenty-First Century.* New York: Afrikan World InfoSystems, 2011.

Yoon-Hendricks, Alexandra, and Theresa Clift. "Up 19%, Homelessness in Sacramento County Hits 5,570. Officials 'Frustrated' but Hopeful." sacbee. The Sacramento Bee, June 26, 2019.
https://www.sacbee.com/news/local/homeless/article231944253.html.

Aime Cesaire, Frantz Fanon, Tupac, and Mozzy: A Colonial Struggle

The hyper-militarization of society is the artifact of colonial domination, whether that be settler colonialism or the vestiges resulting in neocolonial dominance. Militarization of colonial rule has not only been institutionalized by the structures erected during colonialism but has also permeated into the psyche of society; resulting in an adverse psychologic effect on those classified as subordinate upon the creation of race as a social structure within the colonial society and delineated as the native. This perspective is also maintained when analyzing the subordination of imported - enslaved Africans in the settler colony which would become the United States of America. Although they were not native to the land nor possessing the power to be settlers of the "new world", enslaved Africans would resort to the self-determinative violence which Algerian revolutionary Frantz Fanon contended as being necessary by the "native" as a response to violence being exerted by the settler – called decolonization. Frantz Fanon posits their [the settler and the native] first encounter was marked by violence and their existence together--that is to say the exploitation of the native by the settler--was carried on by dint of a great array of bayonets and cannons.[240] In fact, Fanon strongly emphasizes that it is the racial colonizer who is the "bringer of violence into the home and into the mind of the native."[241] Contemporarily, the institutions erected by the perpetrators of settler colonialism are still used to maintain "control" of the settler colonial society. And the psychologic permeation of violence as a form of micro-socioeconomic control in poverty-stricken communities has become normal as violence has been normalized by the surrounding institutions and, therefore the surrounding environment. This can be most explicitly observed in the forms of art that emanate from these conditions. Rap/Hip Hop/Trap encompass a form of storytelling that illustrates the lives and traumas faced by those living in these conditions; conditions which are a result of colonialism - economic, political, social, and most importantly psychologic. This essay will seek to contextualize this beautiful struggle through the thought processes and lyrics of Tupac Shakur and Timothy Patterson - more notoriously known as Mozzy.

Aime Cesaire whom Fanon expanded on in his development of the dialectics of decolonization explains the sickness which is colonialism and its effects on the psyche of both the colonizers and the colonized; he says:

> No one colonizes innocently, that no one colonizes with impunity either; that a nation which colonizes, that a civilization which justifies colonialism – and therefore force – is already a sick civilization, a civilization that is morally diseased…[242] [C]olonization, I repeat, dehumanizes even the most civilized man; that colonial activity, colonial enterprise, colonial conquest, which is based on contempt for the native and justified by that contempt, inevitably tends to change him who undertakes it; that the colonizer, who in order to ease his conscience gets into the habit of seeing the other man as an animal, accustoms himself to treating himself into an animal. It is this result, this boomerang effect of colonization…[243]

As a result, Cesaire argues that the deracination of Africans [under colonialism] must be countered and/or combatted by a "violent affirmation" of their Africanity, which

---

[240] Frantz Fanon. *The Wretched of the Earth. Pref. by Jean-Paul Sartre.* p.36
[241] Ibid., p.38
[242] Aime Cesaire. *A Discourse on Colonialism: Transl. by Joan Pinkham.* p.17-18
[243] Ibid., p.19-20

includes not only their distinct identity but also their unique historicity.[244] This is where Fanon asserts that the violence taken up by the native is a reaction to having no choice but to claim their humanity, in which he asserts: The racially colonized, "back... to the wall... knife... at [Their] throat[s]," realizes that exists but one way out of the wicked, white supremacist colonial world "the settlers" have made, and that is "gun in hand," "ready for violence at all times."[245] However, this violence does not solely affect the physical nature of the native; colonial domination and violence shapes the perception of internal and external lived experiences of the colonized. What Dr. Frances Cress Welsing identifies as the permeation of white supremacy in every aspect of society within the United States, Fanon argues that it is racial colonial violence (white supremacy) which permeates the social fabric of society under colonialism. Reiland Rabaka in a summation of Fanon contends:

Violence is not simply physical; there are also psychological dimensions to violence. What is more, racial colonial violence is extremely predatory and pervasive and seeks to racialize and colonialize many aspects of the racially colonized's life-worlds and lived-experiences, as many elements of their history and culture, as it inhumanly and possibly can: from politics to economics, education to religion, psychology to social organization, aesthetics to ethics, and into oblivion.[246]

In the discourse of International Relations, there is heavy emphasis on ensuring states do not encroach upon the sovereignty of other states. The basic definition of what constitutes a state's sovereignty is its ability to maintain a monopoly of control over violence within its borders. This is done by burgeoning both preemptive and reactionary violent institutions that are used to control the violence introduced to society as a result of colonialism. Thus, society must concede that violence (institutional and psychological) is inherent within sovereign states, especially those created out of colonialism. Herbert Marcuse supports:

Even in the advanced centers of civilization, violence usually prevails: it is practiced by the police, in the prisons and mental institutions, in the fight against racial minorities, it is carried by the defenders of metropolitan freedom, into the backward countries. This violence, indeed, breeds violence.[247]

Viviane Saleh-Hannah while living and studying the effects of colonialism on the penal system in Nigeria realized that the violence which was brought to Nigeria as a result of colonial domination has its vestiges not only in the physical form of police brutality and mass incarceration, but socially within aspects of the family structure. Dr. Kayode Fayemi introduces the perspective which Biko Agozino and Unyierie Idem substantiate upon that show how the societal vestiges of colonial rule permeate the institution of the family, the educational system, the economy, the military, the judiciary, traditional communities, and the collective psyche of the Nigerian people.[248] "[We] observed the militarization of family and kinship relations, with men assuming a militaristic attitude towards women and children, resulting in widespread domestic violence, abuse, and anti-democratic tendencies in civil society."[249] [Their research] concludes that their psyche has become so militarized that it "now embraces force and routine violence..."[250] Their conclusion is parallel to the

[244] Reiland Rabaka. *Forms of Fanonism: Frantz Fanons Critical Theory and the Dialectics of Decolonization.* p.111
[245] Reiland Rabaka. *Forms of Fanonism: Frantz Fanons Critical Theory and the Dialectics of Decolonization.* p.134
[246] Ibid..., p.134
[247] Ibid..., p..276
[248] Viviane Salwh-Hanna, and Chris Affor. *Colonial Systems of Control: Criminal Justice in Nigeria.* p.69
[249] Ibid..., p.72
[250] Ibid..., p.70

lived experiences of Black people living in the settler colony known as the United States, and in poverty. These propensities will be illustrated by the stories of trauma illustrated by Tupac and Mozzy.

If the psychologic effects of colonialism are still apparent in Nigeria despite the ostensible withdrawal (ostensible because they left their institutions) of British rule, then the psychologic effects of violence within a settler colony that is the United States should surely be superfluous.

What is often called "Black on Black" crime is really the result of colonial condition forcing Black people into existential deprivation while increasing interaction with settler colonial systems of control, otherwise known as law enforcement agencies. These systems which derive their legitimacy from colonial violence and continue to rely on reactionary violence as punishment for violation of colonial law. This occurs while "natives" in this colonial society have to unwittingly deal the permeation of violence in their daily interactions.

At a young age Tupac understood class relations and the disparities within capitalism that cause widespread poverty. Like Fanon, Tupac was able to contextualize the discourse of Marx and his analysis of the working and ruling class and "stretch it" as Fanon would say to fit the lived experiences of Black people living in poverty. Through his music Tupac tells stories of these lived experiences and during his interviews, he contextualizes what can be perceived as the result of colonial domination on the lives of the most alienated population in the periphery of the colonial economy; quoting him below:

> *And My raps that I'm rapping to my community shouldn't be filled with rage? You know what I'm saying they shouldn't be filled with the same atrocities that they gave to me? And the media they don't talk about it, so in my raps I have to talk about it, and it just seems foreign because there's no one else talking about it.*

> *"I want to see a true picture. I don't care if [a Rap critic] feels uncomfortable. 'Cause what about when I felt uncomfortable for 400 years? Now, all of a sudden it's bad to talk about [reality]…what we're doing is using our brains to get out of the ghetto any way we can. So we tell these stories, and they tend to be violent. Because our world tends to be filled with violence…that's all my music is about: the oppressed rising up against the oppressor. So the only ones that's scared are the oppressors." (1992)*

> *We as rappers brought the violence that we saw on the streets and put it on our records. We put it on our records for years. And after three, four years, people are finally starting to see it [and review] the statistics that's goin' on in the streets. (1994)*

> *"[Irresponsibility with lyrics] is you talk about murder and death, but you don't talk about the pain. Or you talk about killin', and robbin', and stealin', but you don't talk about jail, death, and betrayal, and all the things that go with it." (1995)*

Within these quotes Tupac references colonial domination, he gives a Marxian metaphoric example of the dialectics of revolution, he details the trauma experienced living in these conditions and how this manifest into the music emanating from this environment, as well as the lived experiences forging the internal conflicts that perpetuate the violence in these communities. These same characteristics are found within Mozzy's music, and it is no coincidence that Mozzy looked to Tupac as influence when creating his music. It is this reason why he paid tribute to Tupac by referencing him in a multitude of songs – even reproducing songs like *Thugz Mansion* and releasing it on the date of Tupac's death. In an interview with the *Grammy Awards* Mozzy explains the impact of Tupac on his life and in his music:

> *It was important for me to pay tribute to Pac because he's legendary. He's my biggest influence as far as musically, politically; he's my mentor. I, still to this day, vibe to his music. I throw it in the deck, I listen to his speeches. So you now, that's one of my biggest influences. I don't think I'd be the rapper that I am today, or as creative as I am if it wasn't for Pac… I was in tears in one of his song, "Dear Mama." I just identified with that song, just crazy how I identified with that song, just seeing the video. My grandmother, Tupac fan, loves Pac. You know, there aren't too many rappers that she like, you feel me? She loved Pac, so he has always been in the household, everybody in my family [loved him], my uncle got thug life tatted on him, you feel me? But early on I used to read books about him and just how hard he worked, how consistent, how persistent he was, and I vowed, I vowed to follow that trait. I vowed to adopt that trait and his work ethic, just his work ethic and the amount of projects he put out.[251]*

It is clear after listening to multiple songs that Mozzy has a great understanding of the circumstances faced by himself and others like him. Delineating the beautiful struggle, he often tells a story of how the circumstances in his life affected his conscious and the pain incited as a result; however, he also the highlights the beauty in the struggle and how it affected his perception of the circumstances.

> *It's a beautiful struggle*
> *I had to watch my mama suffer*
> *They just popped my lil brother*
> *It's a beautiful struggle*
> *My lil sister on duffle*
> *Cuz her babydaddy a hustler*
> *It's a beautiful struggle*
> *I promise to come from nothing*
> *But they make sure that I aint want for nothing*
> *It's a beautiful struggle*
> *I say beautiful because I love it*
> *After this we aint doing no more struggling*
> *Move you out of the struggle…[252]*

---

[251] Ana Yglesias. "Mozzy On 'Thugz Mansion," Tupac's Influence & More."
[252] Timothy Patterson. "Beautiful Struggle," track 2 on *Beautiful Struggle*

This shit brazy cuz my own niggas want me to fail
My baby mama geekin – bitch want me in jail
Twin Mozzy keep calling
He need some dough for his bail…
The pigs lock me up whenever they run the check
Fugitive slave act in full affect
I told em Ima man but they consider me less
And this the shit as a people we don't address
And my wrong or right consciously niggas is still oppressed
I'm overdosing on oil when I be stressing
The blind lead the blind without a sense of direction
And it's a blessing just to live this long
Brutality from the law this shit been going on…[253]

---

[253] Timothy Patterson. "Tappin Out," track 6 on *Beautiful Struggle*

I lost my lil' brother, right that shit hurt
But even worse, he helped send Miguel to jail
That nigga died on paperwork
Pull up to the grave site, woozy of an eight of syrup
You'll never know what I go through as a man
Let my mama down when she needed a helping hand...
The dream died Dr. King got blamed
Tryna stand up for us, now look at where we stand
Black on Black crime a part of them people plan...[254]

---

[254] Timothy Patterson. "The People Plan," track 1 on *Fake Famous*

I been thinking about my past, and what I had to do
Please don't judge me, but this jungle full of animals
They took my nigga, and my nigga, shit I had to move…
My environment be slimy, Ima living product…
I swear I love life, but I've been living heartless.[255]

[255] Timothy Patterson and E Mozzy. "Perkys Callin'," track 3 on *Fraternal Twins 2*

I do the wocky with the Ice, you couldn't knock me for my habits
Gotta family full of addicts, my life a lil dramatic.
I pray I see tomorrow, I'm knowing that my time here is borrowed...[256]

[256] Timothy Patterson. "Borrowed Time," track 3 on *Fake Famous*

Child Protective Services, only thing can break me
Family of a murder victim, only reason you should hate me
I've been feeling smothered lately, bruh called me for the yankee
He aint even call to thank me for that put on I gave him
I miss my brother Deezy, only if the bullets only grazed him
Wasn't no hatred in my heart until that happened, that's what changed me
My last trip to Quinten for that yeeky really saved me...[257]

---

[257] Timothy Patterson. "Sleep Walkin," track 5 on *1 Up Top Ahk*.

They caught me with a thang
Had to do a little time in the cell
I started redefining myself, I think I'm finding myself
You know nothing of this pain that I felt…
My auntie said I need to pray
Lord knows she believe in them better days
We just tryna maintain
You probably went through the same thang
I needed love, that why a nigga gangbang…
It's a number game, I knew you couldn't do the time
Call them from jail, my family like, what you do this time
Before I send my brother to jail, I'd rather do his time…[258]

---

[258] Timothy Patterson. "Finding Myself," track 6 on *Beautiful Struggle*

Conversatin' with the clouds like Ima hold you down
Your mama hardly smiles since she lost a child
She couldn't even view the body without falling out
And every time I hear the line, we just talk about you
She be tellin me all the funny shit I aint know about you
She can only hear your voice is what she once said…
Deray laid bleedin, I remember the smell
Somebody gotta feel what I feel
You done been there before
Can't even count how many niggas is gone
Wish yall was here now that niggas is on
You don't hear me though
You can never understand the way my youngin raised
Try and sympathize but never understand a mother's pain
I hugged my nigga mama when he died
She just started cryin', she cried and she cried
If you could only see the pain in her eyes
Cause he aint coming back, you gotta take it up with god…[259]

---

[259] Timothy Patterson. "Take It Up With God," track 4 on *1 Up Top Ahk*

Gangland baby
I believe in god, but I don't think he can save me
Therefore, I gotta ride around with this yankee
One up in a P80…[260]

---

[260] Timothy Patterson and E Mozzy. "Get It," track 5 on *Fraternal Twins 2*

Mama used to choke slam us just for talkin back
Gangsta rap died with Pac, Mozzy brought it back...
I aint become what mama want me to be
But I told her, learn to love me for me
I hustle for her cause aint nothin for free
Member back we had nothin to eat
Family Bargain Center, Granny was cheap
She'll never spend a hunnid on sneaks
Three bands selling dope all week
That's how I really fell in love with the streets
I fell in love with the streets
Stolo, ride around on E
D.E. got that fire on me
Pull up to the market, I remember putting five on three
Turn around and drop five on the tree
I been high all week
I know some niggas that done died in the streets
It aint too many that survive in these streets
It's suicide in these streets
His mama cried as he lie in these streets
They covered that boy body with sheets
Ima pray for her, hell, aint nothin I can say to her...[261]

[261] Timothy Patterson. "Can't Take It (Ima Gangsta)," track 15 on *1 Up Top Ahk*

What I have delineated as the colonial struggle, Mozzy has called a beautiful struggle. A part of recognizing the conditions faced under colonialism is the beauty in the efforts to change those conditions for the colonized. For Mozzy it has been changing the material conditions for himself, his family, and the people around him who have aided his rise out of the struggle. For revolutionaries, there is beauty in the struggle to decolonize ourselves as well as our environment. Preverbally finding ourselves while immersed in the struggle to change the material conditions of our people while also combatting the institutions who seek to ensure we remain colonized. Mozzy's illustration of the struggle is received and is relatable to many others facing the same circumstances but different geographical locations. Mozzy, much like Tupac recognized the power of storytelling and its ability to transcend geographical borders because of the shared existential lived experiences of people in poverty or in Mozzy's words who come from nothing. There is an innate revolutionary aesthetic in this music because it inherently amalgamates populations who are forced to the periphery of the economy as well as society, and then maintains their position through law enforcement agencies. This is not an attempt to romanticize the immiseration endured by people living under settler colonialism, but it is an explanation of how colonialism affects the lives of "natives" who are not living but merely surviving under this form of domination.

Bibliography

Césaire Aimé. *Discourse on Colonialism: Transl. by Joan Pinkham.* New York: Monthly Review Press, 1972.

Fanon, Frantz. *The Wretched of the Earth. Pref. by Jean-Paul Sartre.* New York: Grove Press, 1968.

Patterson, Timothy. "Beautiful Struggle," track 2 on *Beautiful Struggle,* Mozzy Records 2016, Apple Music.

Patterson, Timothy. "Borrowed Time," track 3 on *Fake Famous,* Mozzy Records 2017, Apple Music.

Patterson, Timothy. "Can't Take It (Ima Gangsta)," track 15 on *1 Up Top Ahk,* Mozzy Records 2017, Apple Music.

Patterson, Timothy. "Finding Myself," track 6 on *Beautiful Struggle,* Mozzy Records 2016, Apple Music.

Patterson, Timothy. "Sleep Walkin," track 5 on *1 Up Top Ahk,* Mozzy Records 2017, Apple Music.

Patterson, Timothy. "Take It Up With God," track 4 on *1 Up Top Ahk,* Mozzy Records 2017, Apple Music.

Patterson, Timothy. "Tappin Out," track 6 on *Beautiful Struggle,* Mozzy Records 2016, Apple Music.

Patterson, Timothy. "The People Plan," track 1 on *Fake Famous,* Mozzy Records 2017, Apple Music.

Patterson, Timothy and E Mozzy. "Get It," track 5 on *Fraternal Twins 2*, Mozzy Records 2016, Apple Music.

Patterson, Timothy and E Mozzy. "Perkys Callin'," track 3 on *Fraternal Twins 2*, Mozzy Records 2016, Apple Music.

Rabaka, Reiland. *Forms of Fanonism: Frantz Fanons Critical Theory and the Dialectics of Decolonization.* Lanham, MD: Lexington Books, 2011.

Saleh-Hanna, Viviane, and Chris Affor. *Colonial Systems of Control: Criminal Justice in Nigeria.* Ottawa: University of Ottawa Press, 2008.

Yglesias, Ana. "Mozzy On 'Thugz Mansion," Tupac's Influence & More."
GRAMMY.com. Recording Academy, September 10, 2019.
https://www.grammy.com/grammys/news/mozzy-talks-thugz-mansion-tupacs-
influencegangland-landlord-more.

Made in the USA
Columbia, SC
06 February 2023

11870426R00062